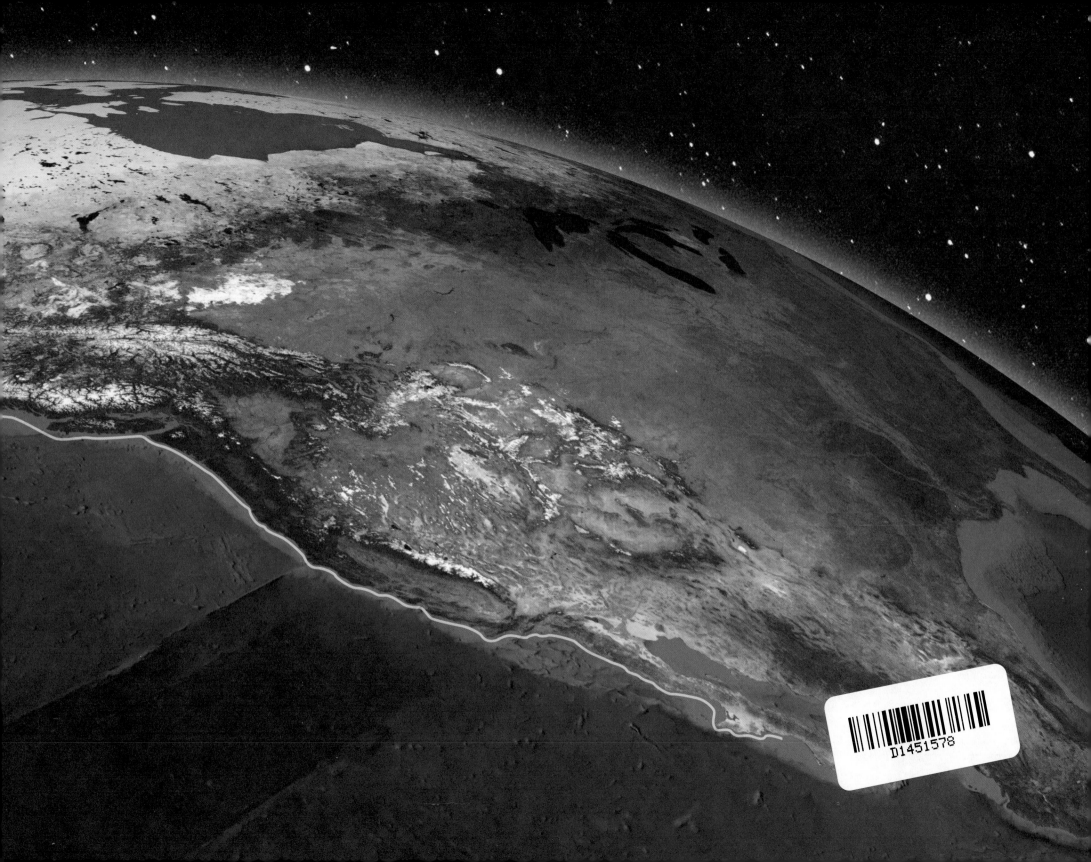

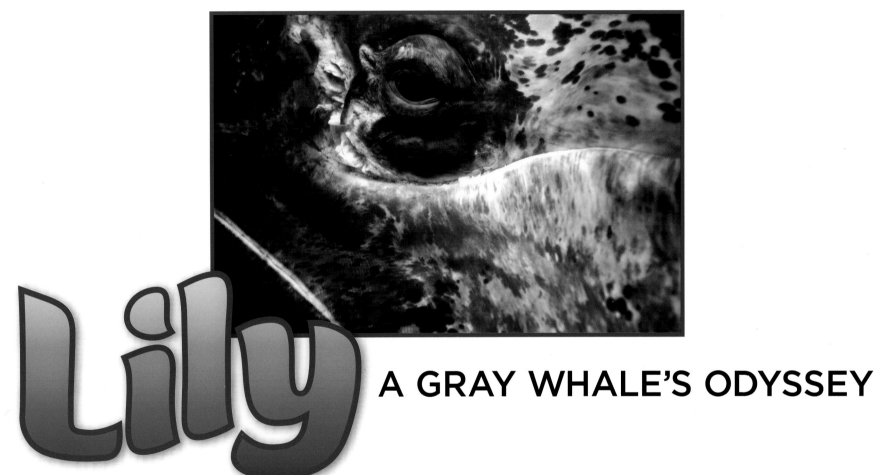

Lily

A GRAY WHALE'S ODYSSEY

By "Capt. Dave" Anderson

Foreword by
Jean-Michel Cousteau

For
My Father in Heaven
Gisele
Arielle
Ann Anderson, mom
Paul Lawrence
Lily

Library of Congress Control Number: 2011961979

ISBN 9780972106818

Printed in the United States of America

Book design by Jeff Girard, Victoria Street Graphic Design

Proofreaders: Lori Verstegen, Dorine Imbach, Tom Miesch, Sandra Maring, Alisa Schulman-Janiger, Amy Mihele

Scientific Advisors:
Robert L. Pitman, NOAA, Protected Resources Division, Southwest Fisheries Science Center, National Marine Fisheries

Edward Lyman, Resource Protection Manager, Large Whale Entanglement Response Coordinator, NOAA, Hawaiian Islands Humpback Whale National Marine Sanctuary

Alisa Schulman-Janiger, American Cetacean Society/Los Angeles Chapter

Other individuals with
The National Oceanic and Atmospheric Administration and
The American Cetacean Society also read and reviewed copy for scientific accuracy.

Lucid Dreamer Productions
San Juan Capistrano, CA 92675

Copies of this book can be purchased by calling 949-488-2828
or visiting www. DolphinSafari.com or www.talesfromthepod.com.
Re-sellers inquiries are welcome.

CONTENTS

I want you to know that most of the major events in this book actually happened. There are some fictional aspects to this story, which I believe will become obvious to readers who wish to separate fact from fiction, but everything else is real, documented, scientifically accurate natural history. In fact, this book was reviewed by experts from the National Oceanic and Atmospheric Administration and others to ensure that the facts given and the non-fictional behaviors of the animals are scientifically accurate. I believe this book will help you see the world from a new perspective, from a gray whale's point of view. You will better understand how these creatures live and die. And you will better understand the many challenges they face.

The photographs in this book are all from real life; none of them were staged or faked. Many of the names of the whales and dolphins were invented by my daughter, Arielle, not to protect them, but because their language consists of whistles, grunts, groans, and clicks, which are completely unpronounceable in our limited human language.

—Captain Dave Anderson

Capt. David Anderson owns and operates Capt. Dave's Dolphin and Whale Safari. Capt. Dave believes the first step in helping to protect whales and dolphins is creating an awareness of how beautifully alive the ocean is, and then giving people an intimate look into the lives and problems these animals face. His film Wild Dolphins and Whales of Southern California won seven awards at the International Wildlife Film Festival. He has also been given awards for his conservation and rescue work with whales and dolphins. Capt. Dave created the first commercial whale watching boat with underwater viewing pods for viewing wild dolphins (and sometimes whales). He made international news by being the first to broadcast whale watching trips live over the internet every day. His sightings, footage, photographs, and encounters with whales and dolphins regularly make local and national news. He has been a featured guest on the NBC Today show, ABC's Eye on LA, the CBS Early Show and more.

Marine mammals are our closest relatives in the sea. They are intelligent, self-conscious, social, and important to the health of ocean ecosystems. I have observed whales and dolphins all around the world and I continue to be amazed by their grace, beauty and complex behavior. Gray whales have been so interesting to me that I produced a PBS documentary on this species entitled "The Gray Whale Obstacle Course." As the title implies, we have not made life easy for these fascinating creatures. They and we are mammals; we are related, and we need to treat our relatives better.

Captain Dave is a personal friend who has also spent a lot of time with gray whales. I applaud his efforts to share the wonder of these whales with kids and the public in general. He has an important story about the challenges gray whales face in this book, *Lily, a Gray Whale's Odyssey*. He is doing important work to help people better understand and appreciate these magnificent whales.

—Jean-Michel Cousteau

Since first being "thrown overboard" by his father at the age of seven with newly invented SCUBA gear on his back, Jean-Michel Cousteau has been exploring the ocean realm. The son of ocean explorer Jacques Cousteau, Jean-Michel has investigated the world's oceans aboard Calypso *and* Alcyone *for much of his life. Honoring his heritage, Jean-Michel founded Ocean Futures Society in 1999 to carry on this pioneering work. He has produced over 80 films, received the Emmy, the Peabody Award, the 7 d'Or, and the Cable Ace Award.*

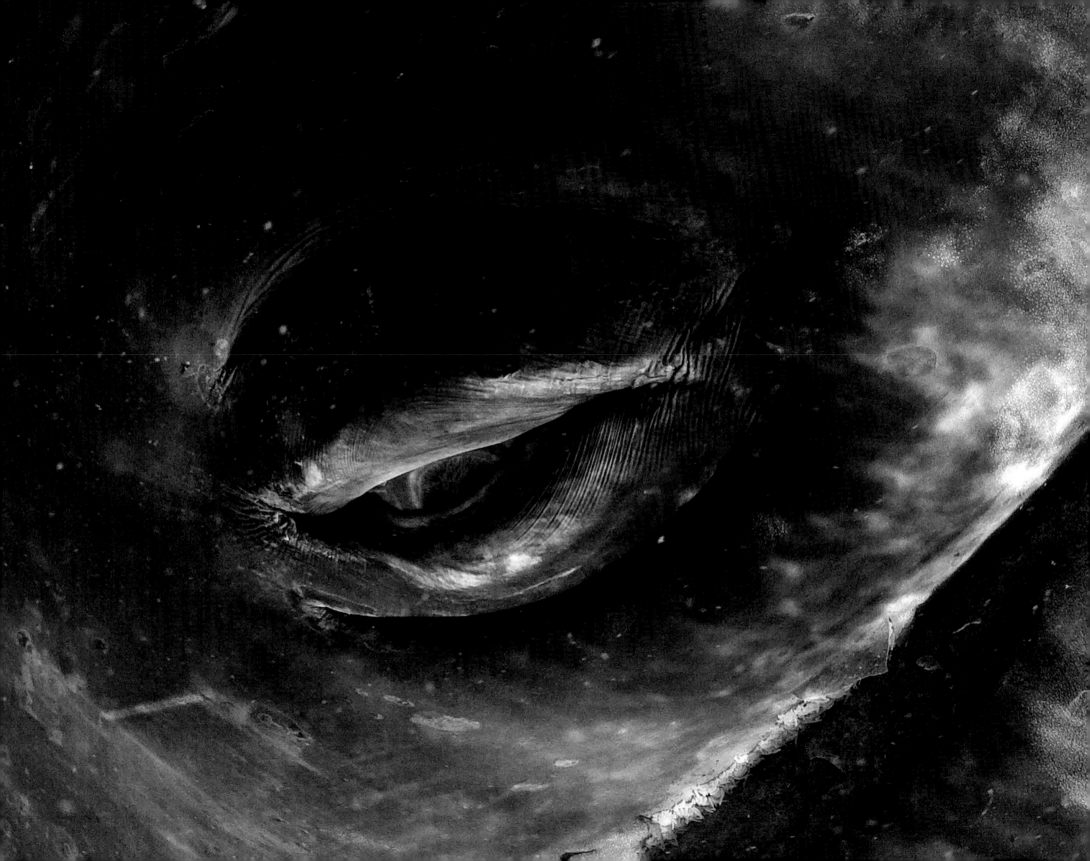

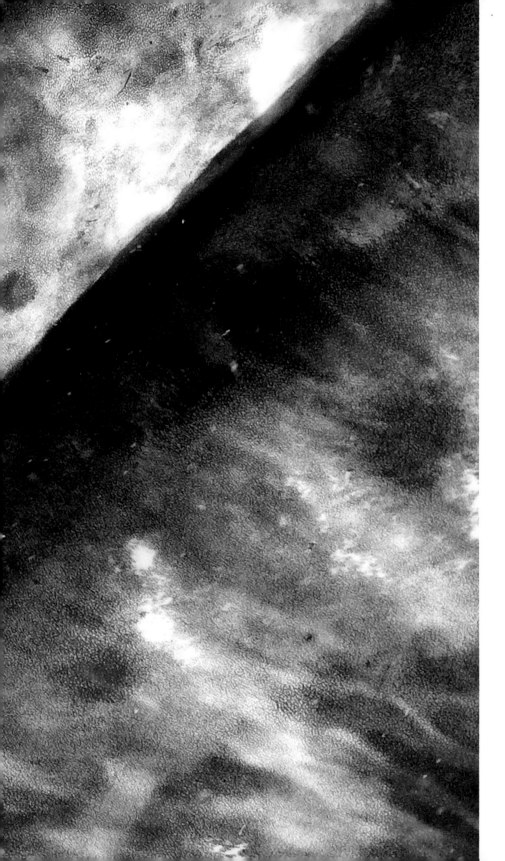

CHAPTER ONE

The Beginning

I know some of you will find this hard to accept, but you must try and if you can, you will believe, and then you will hear the voice of the whale, Lily.

A few years before this book was written, the animals of the ocean were given the ability to communicate with each other: whales to dolphins, to fish to sea lion, and anyone else who believed. They began to tell their stories one to another and to the few humans who believed enough to hear them. They were also given knowledge and because their eyes were opened, the animals of the ocean became like man: free to choose between right and wrong. And their lives were never the same again.

This is one of their stories.

On May 10, 2010, a young, 26-foot California gray whale made its way into Dana Point Harbor south of Los Angeles.

The whale was in serious trouble. People wondered if it needed help, but they didn't know what was wrong. Someone thought they saw a rope caught on the animal's tail flukes, it was hard to tell for certain in the murky water.

Gray whales had entered Dana Point Harbor before, but none had stayed this long—two full days. A crowd of spectators gathered on the shore.

Arielle and her dad, Capt. Dave, sat on the rocks and quietly watched the whale. The giant barely moved as it labored up to the surface to breathe every few minutes. Arielle moved closer to the barnacled creature. She sensed something was wrong, and, being young and unafraid of what others thought, she knelt down on a rock and prayed, "God, please help this poor whale."

Soon she heard a sound, like chains rattling, coming from the whale. It then became recognizable as a voice.

"Oh, little Caretaker, you say you really want to help me. I only wish it were true. But very soon, I think, it will be the harpoon I see," sighed the whale in a raspy whisper. "Only a fool would trust a human, and I am no fool!"

Arielle was surprised to hear the whale's voice, but not overly surprised because she was one of the few people able to understand them. She had been talking to dolphins and whales and other sea creatures for nearly half of her eight years.

"Why don't you trust us?" she asked.

"You can understand me?" the whale questioned.

"Yes. Yes, I can understand you! Do you need help? Are you hurt?" asked Arielle.

"Why do you want to know?"

"So we can help you."

" Yes, so you say. Where are your weapons? Oh, I see," the whale nervously whispered, "that male person over there has a harpoon!"

"No, that's a fishing pole. We're not going to hurt you," Arielle assured.

"Where are the Caretakers in the blue building?" the whale asked.

"How do you know about them?"

"I met someone a long time ago, a tiny human, and she told my mom . . . oh, it does not matter! Why do you want to know anyway?"

"Listen, Whale. I promise we only want to help you."

"Oh, Caretaker, if only . . . look, you are the only one—the only one—I am able to talk to around here." The whale's voice was choked up with emotion, "I desperately need to trust someone."

"What's wrong?" Arielle quietly asked.

"Well, uh, other than the fact that I have a net wrapped around me, and I am weak from hunger, and it hurts ever so much to move, nothing, really." With that the whale began to release the gift of tears.

"Don't cry, Whale. We'll help you. You're going to be okay. My name is Arielle."

"Mine is . . . . (The whale said its name by making popping sounds while quietly sobbing, but there is no translation in our language for these sounds.)

So Arielle thought about it and said, "Okay. Well, how 'bout if we call you Lily? That's what my dad's friend Barry has been calling you."

"Forgive me, Arielle, but I have bigger problems going on here than my name. Please call me anything in your language that suits you, even if it is the name of a female Caretaker."

"Dad, Lily has a net wrapped around her!" Arielle proudly exclaimed to her father.

"She does? Lily, huh? She told you her name?"

"Yeah, sort of," responded Arielle.

"She has a net wrapped around her?" Arielle's father asked. "That is terrible. Well, I'm glad she told you about it."

Her dad was not convinced that Arielle could talk to the animals, but he loved his daughter, so he played along as if he believed.

"Are you going to get it off her?" Arielle asked.

"We will, Honey, but first we'll just sit here and watch her until I can see it for myself."

"Show him, Lily," Arielle pleaded.

Lily tried to raise her tail flukes to show him the netting, but it was too painful, and the muscles and tendons that worked her flukes were badly damaged.

"I can't," Lily moaned.

"What happened to you, Lily? How did you get that net wrapped around you?" questioned Arielle.

"I would like to tell you, but I am afraid you are too young to hear my story. It is too rough for young ears."

"I can handle it, Lily. I'm not a little kid, you know!"

"Are you sure you really want to know?" asked Lily.

"Yes, of course I do!" cried Arielle.

"Then I will tell you the whole story," said Lily, "because to know it in part will not change a thing. I am going to give you my story as a gift, young Caretaker, so that you will give it to the Caretakers who can't hear me. I will tell you so that what happened to me will not happen again to anyone else."

"I will tell your story; I promise!" Arielle raised her hand as she promised.

So, as Capt. Dave and others watched, hoping to spot the netting, Lily began to tell Arielle her story.

Two bottlenose dolphins showed up near Lily and listened to every word spoken, all the while pretending to chase fish nearby.

One of the dolphins eavesdropping on Lily was a very old and very wise dolphin that Arielle had appropriately named Old Dolphin.

CHAPTER TWO

Lily and The Lagoon

Lily began to tell her story:

I was born in The Lagoon in The Warmest Place. It is where my mother was born and her mother, and her mother's mother, and so on. You Caretakers call it San Ignacio Lagoon. I was very little back then, only the length of two tall Caretakers.

My mom said that as soon as I was born, I swam to the surface, real clumsy like, and took my first breath.

FAST FACTS

San Ignacio Lagoon, in Baja California, Mexico, is a biosphere where the whales are completely protected.

A gray whale calf is about 15.09 feet (4.6 meters) long at birth.

15

Mom was always right next to me in those days. Whenever I became hungry, I nursed from her. But Mom never ate anything because there was nothing to eat in the lagoon. She loved to show me off to all our relatives, friends and lagoon mates—the other whales in The Lagoon. They told us many stories about what they had seen or done during that year's migration. She introduced me to the Caretakers who visited us in small panga boats. I was my mom's first calf.

FAST FACTS

A gray whale calf grows at a rate of about fifty pounds a day feeding on mother's milk. But the mother whale, called a cow, is not eating during her stay in the lagoon. She is losing weight every day.

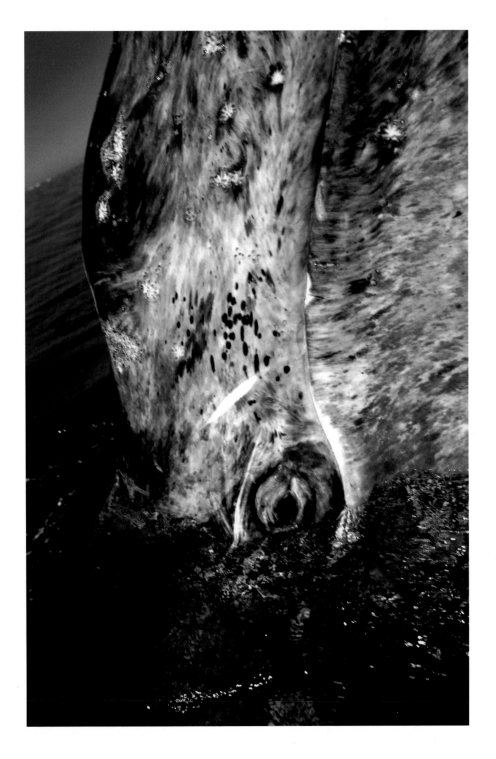

You just wouldn't believe it now, but I was kind of cute back then.

We gray whales use several different lagoons. Some whales visit all of them, but Mom said we should return to the same lagoon every year. It is our winter home, and it is where we try to have our calves.

There were lots of whales in The Lagoon—maybe 300. I loved it there. I always felt very safe and protected. Time in The Lagoon was our whale time, our time to be together, and it was wild and fun. Breaching, spyhopping, courtship, mating, and play were all going on somewhere in The Lagoon. Whales were constantly leaving and arriving, many only staying for a few days. But we did have one spot where everything stayed calm. We called it The Nursery. When it wasn't windy, and the tide was high enough, maybe thirty or forty moms with calves, like my mom and me, would gather there. The moms would sleep in the shallow water while we calves hung out and played nearby.

It was in this nursery that I first met Uncle Mike. Well, actually, I didn't exactly know he was my uncle because my mom sort of ignored him that day. He just kind of showed up and started talking in this fake female whale voice.

"What did one adult male whale in The Nursery say to another adult male whale in The Nursery? Nothing," he said, answering his own riddle, "male whales aren't allowed in The Nursery."

Uncle Mike laughed heartily; then he swam off with all the moms yelling at him to get out. Single whales seldom ventured past the island to where our nursery was.

FAST FACTS

There is a nursery area similar to this in San Ignacio Lagoon where single whales are rarely seen. Aproximately 81 percent of gray whales only stay in this lagoon for a week or less. Many use San Ignacio Lagoon as a staging area before heading north, including cows and calves from other lagoons.

Dana Point
California

BAJA CALIFORNIA

Guerrero Negro

Laguna Ojo de Libre
(Scammon's Lagoon)

Pacific Ocean

The Lagoon
(Laguna San Ignacio)

Magdelena Bay

THE WARMEST PLACE

Uncle Mike loved to tell everyone silly jokes and riddles about sharks and dolphins and whales. The next time I saw him, he swam over to us and, without even saying hello, he asked me a riddle:

"Why does a whale cross the ocean? To get to the other tide. Get it?"

I didn't really get it, but I released the gift of laughter anyway. My mom laughed, too. Then she explained to me how Uncle Mike had made it his purpose to make sure that everyone released that gift as much as possible, ever since it was given to us.

One day Mom got real serious with me. She spyhopped (stuck her head out of the water) and told me to do the same thing. Then she looked me in the eye and gave me this warning:

"You must never forget what I am about to tell you! The Lagoon is the only place we are truly safe, and it is the only place we can completely trust the Caretakers! Do you understand?"

I didn't really understand, but it seemed important to her, so I said yes.

I kept thinking about what she had said until the sun set. The days were short and the nights long in The Lagoon. I realized that it wasn't really what she had said that worried me but, rather, how she had become completely weird when she had said it. But I kind of forgot all about it the next morning when a female Caretaker gave me a huge hug and rubbed my head. I loved having my head rubbed. It felt really good. But it made me sort of wish that I had hands and arms like you Caretakers do. "Caretakers aren't scary," I thought. And I never imagined it could be any different.

FAST FACTS

The birthing lagoons in Baja may be the only places in the world where a "non-researcher" can touch a huge baleen whale in the wild. While gray whales were once hunted almost to extinction in these lagoons, these gentle giants now actually deliberately bring their calves over to strangers of another species to be petted in the same lagoons.

As time passed, one by one, all the whales began to leave the lagoon. The first to leave were the whales that were going to be moms next year in The Lagoon. They left early to begin feeding in The Coldest Place. A couple of weeks later the other adult whales without calves left. Then about a week later, most of the young whales left. Last to leave were moms and calves (like me). After several of them had left, my mom declared, "You are strong enough, Little One. It is time to go to The Coldest Place."

As we left the lagoon, we spotted Uncle Mike and a few other whales body surfing the waves on the sand bar at the mouth of The Lagoon. It looked like fun, and I wanted to try it.

"No," my mom said.

"Why?" I asked.

"Because I said so!" was her reply.

I had heard this a lot, and I knew she would not answer me so I asked Uncle Mike about it. He explained that sometimes whale killers come to the mouth of The Lagoon.

"They never actually go inside the lagoon," he told me, "because there are too many of us around for them to risk it." Then he lowered his voice to a whisper, "Whale Killers are your mom's biggest fear. Personally, just between you, me, and the sea slugs, I think she is being overly protective!"

Just then Mom came back. We said a quick goodbye to Uncle Mike, and off we went. We didn't know it that day, but something just as deadly as the whale killers was waiting for us up ahead.

FAST FACTS

Gray whales can be found bodysurfing outside the entrance to San Ignacio Lagoon, some going back over and over to ride the waves.

24

CHAPTER THREE

Whale Traps

We traveled day and night up the coast, usually staying very close to shore. We were alone most of the time, just Mom and me, plus the occasional whale or dolphin we would run into. For several days we didn't see any sign of boats, or even any Caretakers. It was peaceful, but a little lonely after all the activity in The Lagoon. That's when Mom started telling me more about the Whale Killers. "They are our brothers," she explained, "but they are never to be trusted. Some of them will be waiting up ahead to attack us!" She told me that we always had to watch out for them, especially when we swam over the Deep Canyon, which we would reach soon, and when we traveled through The Dangerous Pass just before The Coldest Place.

FAST FACTS

Monterey Bay, California, and False Pass near Unimak Island, Alaska, are places where killer whales often attack and feed on migrating gray whales.

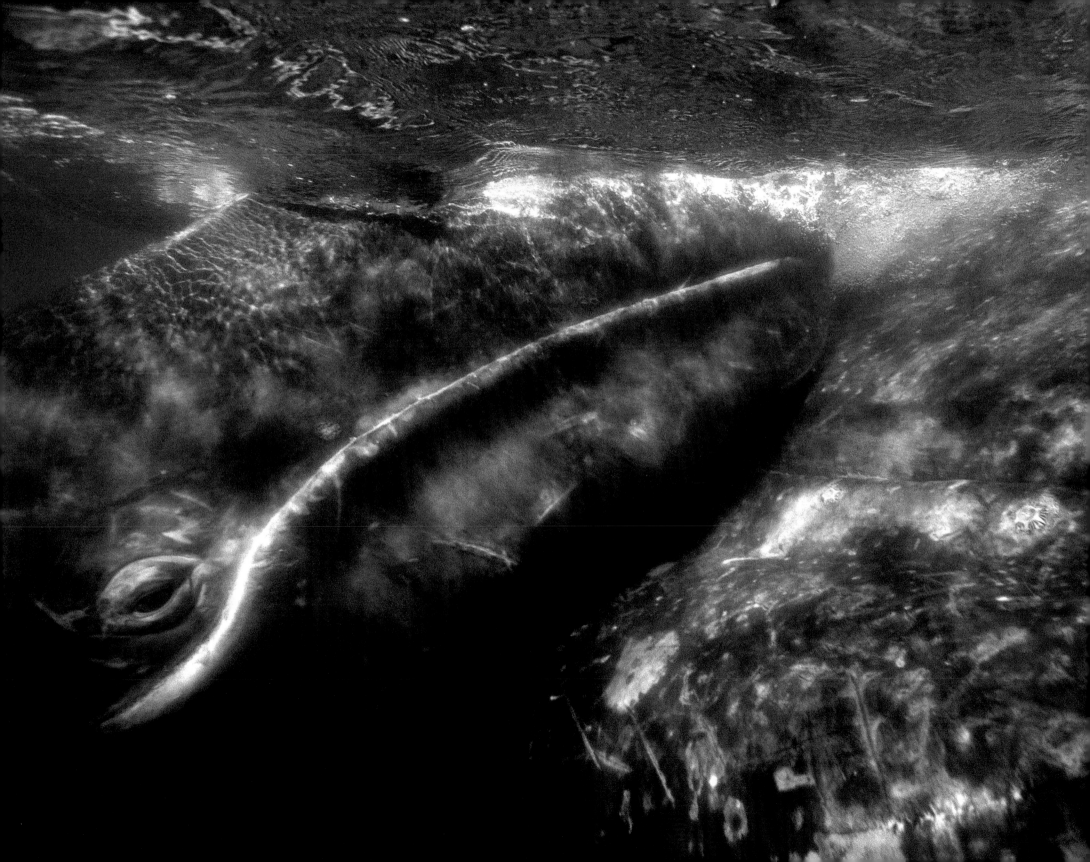

"Are we almost there yet?" I would ask my mom every single day as we swam up the coast, but she never answered the question.

Each morning after the sun would rise, she would breach out of the water, look up the coast, and say, "You see that point of land way up ahead? We'll try to make that spot before the sun is straight overhead." ...and usually we did.

In the afternoon, she would breach again and pick another spot that we needed to reach before the end of the day.

Just before sunset, she'd throw her giant self out of the water again, pick a spot way in the distance and say, "We should be twice that far by sunrise. One flip of the flukes at a time," she would always say. "Each day has enough trouble of its own. Don't worry about tomorrow, Little One. Tomorrow will worry about itself!"

As a result, I never knew how far we were from The Coldest Place, or how much longer it would take to get there.

So, every night I would ask her again, "Are we almost there yet?" But she never answered me.

Sometimes I would spot something I had never seen, and I'd wander off to investigate. Then Mom would swim alongside me and get me back on track. As we swam, we would usually try to stay in about the same depth; about twice as deep as my mom was long (in other words, two Mom-lengths deep). That kept us from getting too close to shore or too far out to sea. It was an easy way to help guide us, even in the pitch black dark.

FAST FACTS

Gray whales average about 75 miles every 24 hours on their migration. They breach for many reasons: to look around, to remove something irritating (like parasites) from their skin, to let others know of their presence, and, sometimes, just for the sheer joy of it.

We started seeing humans setting traps for us. These traps (you call them nets) are supposed to catch fish, but we call 'em whale traps because they catch so many of us. Mom tried to steer me clear of them, but at night in the black water they became invisible.

We kept moving night and day. Unlike you Caretakers, we can keep swimming even when we are asleep, though we stop and take short naps sometimes. I stayed right up against Mom most of the time at night, but sometimes we would get separated and have to find each other. That was always scary!

One night just after sunset, I became separated from my mother. I panicked and started swimming fast in the direction I had last seen her. Suddenly, I felt something brush against my face. I stopped and turned and tried to tear away from it, but I became even more tangled up. I turned and turned and twisted and turned, but that only got me more entangled. I was trapped! I tried with everything I had to push past the trap, but it became harder and harder for me to move. I couldn't even reach the surface to breathe. I pulled and twisted and thrashed! I was totally running out of air! Something had slipped into my mouth. I felt myself beginning to pass out, so I gave one final burst with all I had left in me, and that something in my mouth finally broke loose. I could move again. I pushed to the surface and sucked in air! I was never so happy in my life as I was taking that breath! I was free!

FAST FACTS

Dolphins and whales are believed to sleep with only half their brain at a time. They are voluntary breathers, People are involuntary breathers. Whales and dolphins have to think when they take a breath, or they could breathe in water and drown.

Well, I was almost free! I could swim and breathe, all right, but I still had a dreadful rope in my mouth and a bunch of net wrapped around my tail flukes. With every movement I made, I could feel the net. This obnoxious thing kept tugging at me, kept me from moving normally, and kept rubbing into my skin.

It hurt every time I lifted my tail flukes up and down to swim. Mom found me, looked the net over and tried to untangle it. She had me turn this way and that, but since we don't have arms or hands like you Caretakers do, it was pointless. All we have are flippers, and they are only good for steering us. We don't even have teeth with which to chew the net off, only baleen for filter feeding. So, after a few hours without getting a single scrap of it off, she just gave up. That was the only time I have ever seen my mom cry.

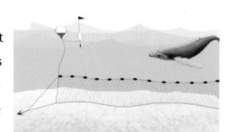

FAST FACTS

Gillnets are one of the worst nets for whale and dolphin entanglement. This is how a gillnet works; floats on top keep it afloat and weights on bottom make it hang down like a curtain. Sometimes the net is anchored to the boat, sometimes not. The fish tries to swim through the net and gets caught by its gills.

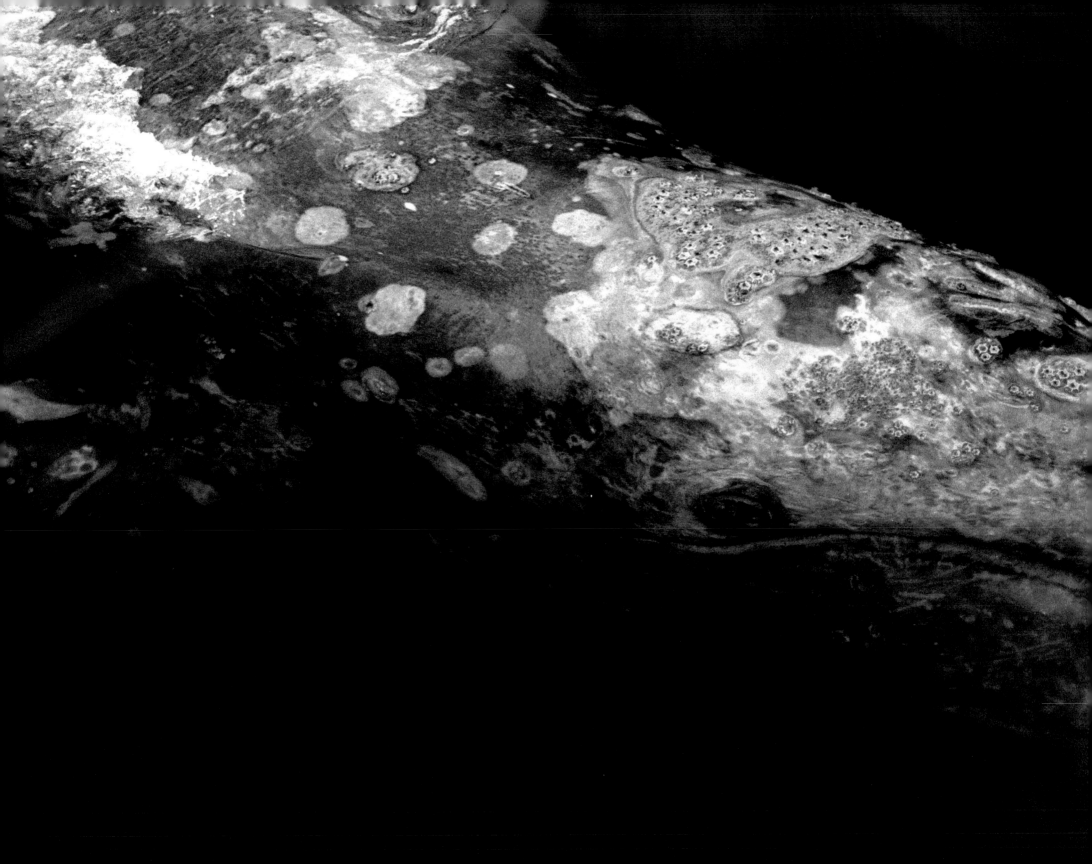

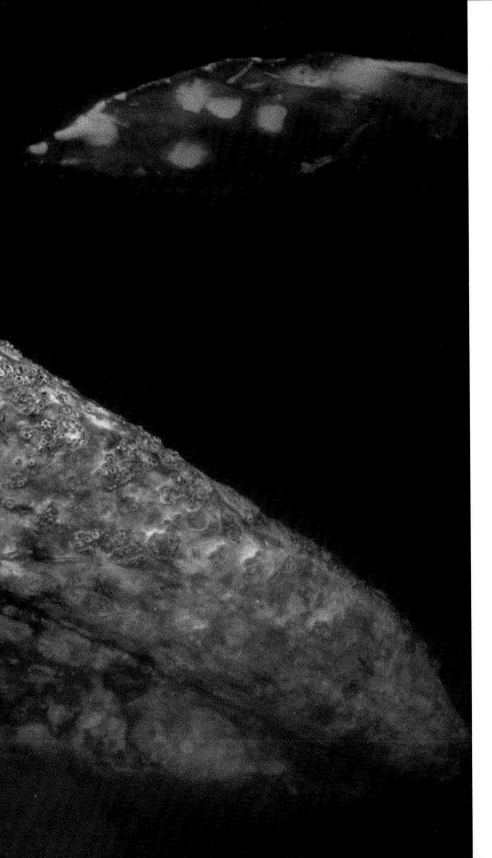

CHAPTER FOUR

Whale Killers

So on we traveled toward our summer home in The Coldest Place, where there is plenty of food. I followed my beautiful mother, trying to match every beat of her tail flukes. She knew the way, and something inside me, something I did not yet understand, knew the way, too.

FAST FACTS

Whales instinctively know which direction to migrate. They may use biomagnetic orientation, but no one knows for certain how they navigate. Gray whales seem to use the underwater depth contours to help guide them.

35

One day we passed by your harbor and an unusual boat with dolphins and words painted on it sailed over us. It had see-through sides and we could see the Caretakers looking at us through the glass hull. It was like they were underwater with us! I started talking to a young female Caretaker through the glass.

"Lily, that was me!" Arielle declared. "It had to be! We are the only ones in the world who have a boat like that! I was in one of the underwater viewing pods. You were just a baby whale back then, right?"

"Oh, of course, it *was* you!" exclaimed Lily. "You are the reason I came into the harbor. I remembered what you told my mother about the Caretakers in the blue building! Yes, Arielle, a year ago I was a young calf. Listen to me, little Caretaker, a lifetime can happen in only one year," Lily said sadly.

"My mom never trusted Caretakers outside of the lagoon, but she was so desperate to help me that this one time she approached your boat all fearless like."

"Yes," said Arielle. "I remember. She came right up to the window of our boat and said, 'Excuse me, but my little calf has a net wrapped around her, and I heard from another whale that you Caretakers might be able to help her.'

"I told her that my dad could help. He was just trained to do so in that big blue building in the harbor."

My Mom was so happy when she heard this that she breached for joy
at just the possibility that I would be free soon.

She leaped out of the water, over and over again.

She even breached right outside of your harbor. I have never seen
her breach so many times. When Mom was really happy, she always
breached.

Her joy spread to me so I joined her in a breach! I jumped as much as I could with all that net and rope pulling on me. Just then we heard a high-pitched whistle under the water. Terror filled Mom's eyes, and though I didn't know the reason, I knew right away that we had to go, so I followed her.

As we bolted past a whistle buoy with California sea lions on it, I could hear the woo-woo sound the buoy made as it bobbed up and down in the swell. I heard a gull cry out from atop the buoy, "Orca! Orca! I think we need a bigger buoy!" Then he laughed like only a gull can laugh.

I saw several sea lions with their flippers out of the water warming themselves near the crowded buoy. As soon as they heard that gull cry "Orca!" they scrambled onto the buoy like seagulls on a sardine.

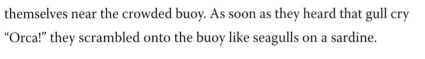

FAST FACTS

California sea lions keep their flippers out of the water to heat or cool themselves. This is called thermoregulation.

I swam as fast as I could after Mom, but with all that netting on me, I could barely keep up. We almost ran into one of the fleeing sea lions.

We headed straight for the kelp.

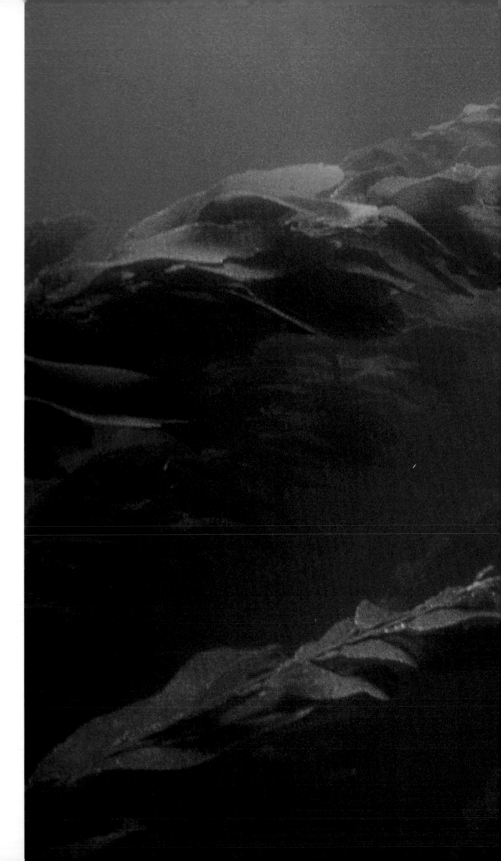

Hiding in the kelp, my mom looked me over then whispered, "Whale Killers."

Caretakers call them killer whales. Killer whales are not just big playful dolphins—they are our greatest fear. Greater than the Caretaker hunters who live in The Coldest Place, because they can show up almost anywhere, like the whale traps. Unlike the whale traps, they chase after us! These enormous dolphins, like all whales with teeth, can find us by making sound pictures. Hiding in the kelp makes it harder for them to spot us, so that's where we stayed! I was too young to be afraid for long, so I started playing with the kelp. My mom made me stop, scolded me and warned me that danger was still close.

FAST FACTS

Killer whales are the largest dolphins. Dolphins and other toothed whales like sperm whales can find things underwater by sending out a series of clicks that bounce back to them. This mechanism is called echolocation. Baleen whales, like Lily and her mom, do not have this same ability to echolocate. However, they may be able to make a loud sound and then listen to hear how long it takes for it to bounce back, thus giving them an approximate depth.

46

Then the Killers showed up!

I heard someone—it must have been your dad —say over the loud-speaker, "These may be transient killer whales, the kind that eat mammals, like sea lions or even these gray whales we've been following. It is hard to say for sure, but if they are resident killer whales, these whales are safe because they only eat fish."

"Yes," said Arielle, "I remember I was so scared for you and your mom."

"Then those killer whales came right over by our boat! One of them swam over to the boat and circled us. So I climbed down into one of the underwater viewing pods and he came right up to me!

"'So,' I asked him, 'Are you chasing after those gray whales to eat them?'"

"'Unfortunately, yes,' the killer whale told me. 'It is not *my* desire to do this. I've tried, but I cannot persuade the other members of my pod to turn from the old ways. We have hunted whales, dolphins, and sea lions for generations, and my pod-mates are unwilling to change. They deny the truths we learned when our eyes were opened.'"

"He swam away before I could ask him anything else," said Arielle. "They were headed straight for the kelp where you were hiding— I thought they would find you for sure!"

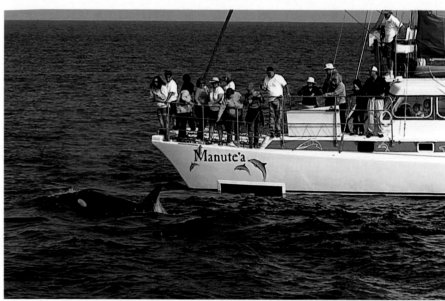

While you were talking to the killer whale, a really old bottlenose dolphin and a young tough-looking dolphin entered the kelp. They swam over to us and the old dolphin whispered, "Don't move and do not make a sound." He got real still, hunched down on the sandy ocean floor, closed his eyes and started concentrating intensely. The weirdest sound we've ever heard came out of that dolphin. It was a high-pitched whistle that sounded like a loud Caretaker's scream. He did it three times. Then all four of us waited underwater till we ran out of air. And when we surfaced, all the Killers were gone.

"It's a new trick going around the dolphin-net." said the elderly bottle-nose. "We imitate a danger sound the Killers make. When they hear that sound it means that another killer has spotted danger and everyone should leave immediately. It's going to get harder for those Dolphin Killers to make a meal out of us dolphins."

"Can you teach it to us?" I asked him.

"No. Sorry, you twin-hole heads cannot make this type of sound, no matter how much you try."

"Why did you help us?" my mom demanded. "What if those Killers found out you tricked them? Since when does a dolphin risk his life for a gray whale!"

"It was the right choice," said the old dolphin, "and that is all that keeps us from being self-centered beasts." We thanked them both by rubbing up against them, which I think frightened them a little because we are so much bigger than them. Then the wise, old dolphin whispered to us, "Take care, my friends, those Killers are still very hungry." They both left without the younger dolphin ever saying a word.

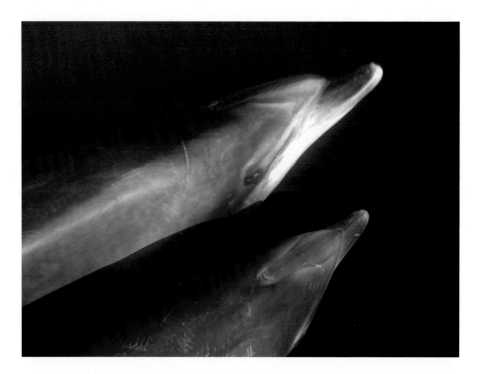

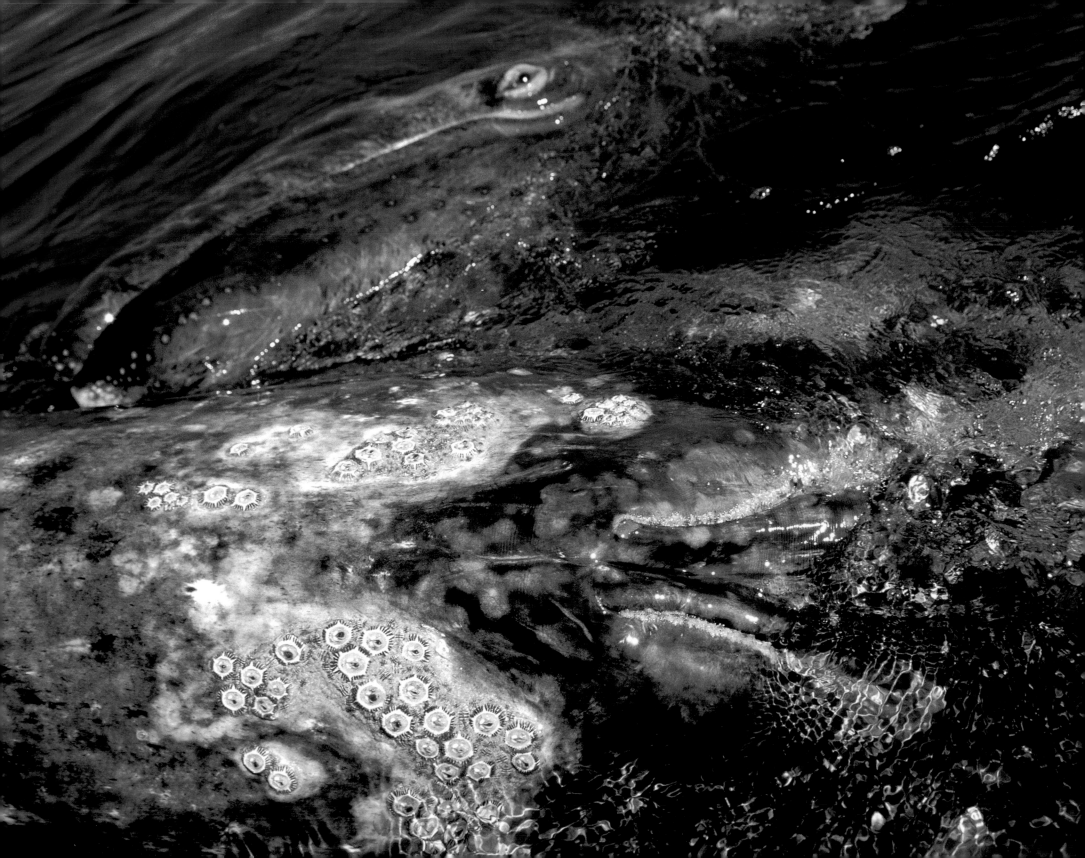

My mom was convinced that the Killers would be waiting for us if we returned to your dad for help, so we kept moving up the coast.

As we made our way, we were keenly aware of everything, but we never saw any sign of the Killers.

Five days later we reached the edge of the deep-water canyon that you Caretakers call Monterey Bay, and my mom said to me, "This is a dangerous place! We will swim fast through here—no resting, no stopping, no fooling around." But we never had time to follow her plan, because the instant we started across that underwater canyon, seven Killers showed up! They toyed with us, swimming dangerously close, silent without a word spoken between them, or to us. They were testing us to see what we would do. My mom tried to look like she wasn't scared, but I could see in her eye that this was it, the moment she feared most. My heart was pounding in my head. I felt weak, like just giving up and surrendering to them, but there would be no mercy from *these* whales.

FAST FACTS

Resident killer whales feed on fish and do not eat mammals; for them this is a natural, normal behavior. Transient killer whales feed on mammals like whales, dolphins, sea lions, and others. As far as anyone knows, they have never killed a human in the wild. For them, also, this is a natural, normal behavior.

Then, without any warning, they came at us. My mom tried her best to keep them away from me by slashing them with her powerful tail flukes. She could have easily overpowered them one at a time. But when the Killers all charged at once, it was too much for her.

One of them slammed into me hard, knocking the breath out of me. Then another bit into my flipper and pulled me under the water until my mom knocked *him* silly with her flukes and he released me. I soon figured out something my mom had deliberately kept from me; it was me they were after!

I was easy prey, much smaller and weaker than the Killers. My mom was too big and strong for them to take down easily without getting hurt. I stayed as close to my mother as I could.

FAST FACTS

NOAA estimates as many as thirty-five percent of gray whale calves may be killed by killer whales.

They kept coming at me from the right and the left. I'm sure they could see the panic in my eyes.

I pushed myself on top of my mom's body to get out of reach of the Killers. I rolled and rolled on top of my last hope— her living, breathing island of safety.

I still was not out of their reach. One of them grabbed ahold of my flipper again with its teeth and pulled me off my Mom. The Killer started pressing down on me, pushing me down before I could take a breath.

I was already so exhausted from them chasing me. I desperately needed air, but I could never quite catch my breath. They tried again and again to get on top of me, to push me under the water, to drown me. Then, right in that moment as I felt my life slipping away, something happened I cannot explain.

One of the Whale Killers, who had been watching nearby as the others attacked, raced toward me! He pressed his body against mine. I could feel his smooth skin.

"Don't worry," this killer whale told me. "No one will touch you now. I am your friend! I will protect you with my life if necessary!"

[As Lily remembered this, her voice trembled with emotion.]

The other Killers circled us and finally began to speak. They cruelly taunted and teased him, like I have never seen.

"Coward!" they called out. "You're a whale kisser, not a Whale Killer! Why don't you marry that barnacled, mud-sucking, twin-hole head?!"

My brave protector shouted back to them, "Is she not a whale like you? Does this whale not breathe air like we do? Does she not swim like us? Is she not intelligent, like some of us? Are we no better than the gulls that would peck the eyes out of a brother gull for food?"

"It is our nature, you fool!" one of the Killers shouted back.

"A fool," retorted my guardian, "finds no pleasure in understanding, but delights in his own opinions. You have been given knowledge—your eyes have been opened! Now you can follow your appetites, or you can do what you now know is right!" he said.

After a few more half-hearted insults, they left us alone, and we swam away from there as fast as we could. This Whale Killer—Buddy, I called him—followed us up the coast for the rest of the day to make sure we were safe, then he disappeared. I really don't know why he did it, but I am only alive because of his actions, and that is the truth of it.

"I think your 'Buddy' was the same killer whale I talked to in our Eye Pod!" Arielle exclaimed.

"I'm sure of it," replied Lily confidently.

CHAPTER FIVE

All Scratched Up

One good thing that happened as a result of the Killers attacking us is that I lost some of the fishing gear; most of the lines and buoys came off in all the action. The net that was left on my flukes was almost invisible, but the pain was ever present.

Our flippers and flukes had lots of bite marks from those Killers, but that wasn't the only scar they left on me. I never felt safe again. I always felt as if something horrible was about to happen. As if at any minute those killer whales or others would pounce on us again.

Day after day, night after night, I followed my mother, staying right next to her. The netting was a constant pest, like barnacles or lice, only a thousand times worse.

My mom and I kept heading up the coast. Whatever it was that was guiding us also urged us to keep moving.

Along the way Caretakers in boats would stop and watch us. They would almost always scream when we showed them our flukes, or breached, or got close to them. Some boats had hundreds of people, and some only a few.

I tried not to complain as Mom kept the pace, but sometimes it hurt so badly when I was swimming that we had to stop and rest.

At one of the places we stopped, we surfaced to find a pod of Killers just ahead of us. It was the first time I had seen any since the canyon attack and, believe me, I was always looking. Killers can show up anywhere, like the nets you Caretakers set. Anyway, mom pushed me into shallow water right away, into the kelp. We held our breath and waited.

I heard an eagle on a buoy nearby screech, "Orca! Orca! I think we need a bigger buoy." The eagle laughed a scary kind of laugh, like only an eagle can do. The steller sea lions on the buoy looked around frightened. When they spotted the orca feeding on salmon, they put their heads down and went back to sleep, unconcerned.

"We're okay. They're Fisheaters." Mom declared.

So we emerged from the kelp and kept moving up the coast.

Right after that, Mom found a spot where there was an abundance of krill. Krill is usually hard for us to catch, but she was so hungry that we stayed there for hours. She swam through swarms of the tiny shrimp-like krill on the surface with her mouth open, and spit the water out through her baleen.

After that, I saw what I thought was blood gushing out of my mom. I was really scared until I remembered that the krill she had been feeding on were red. She had just made the biggest poop I have ever seen in my life!

A sea otter that was floating downwind of us in the kelp shouted out, "Peee yoooo! Hey, maybe a little less krill and a little more amphipods in the diet, my friend!"

Mom and I released the gift of laughter so loud and for so long that my Uncle Mike would have been proud of us.

We kept seeing new and unusual animals in the water and on the shore; some I had never seen before. One day we saw a big brown bear eating clams on a beach. I wanted to investigate but my mom told me to stay away from bears.

As we moved up the coast, we stopped whenever we found something edible in a big enough concentration to make it worthwhile for Mom to feed. We never stayed anywhere too long because my mom kept saying that we would have plenty to eat once we reached The Coldest Place.

CHAPTER SIX

The Coldest Place

One afternoon we passed by some humpback whales that were diving down to feed on herring. Sooty shearwater seabirds were sitting on the water as thick as sardines. A short time later, we felt the current strengthen and pull us toward shore. That was when my mom stunned me with these words, "We are almost there!"

But first we had to go through The Dangerous Pass where Killers often wait for us. Mom had been attacked there when she was a calf, so this place held many bad memories for her. We waited at the entrance for a while in order to allow some other gray whales to catch up.

While we were waiting, the wind began to blow until it was screaming at us. This screaming breeze blew the tops off the waves, so whenever we surfaced to breathe, frigid waves would crash over us. It was hard to even take a breath without sucking in water. Fortunately, under the water all was calm. After a long wait, two female whales with calves caught up with us and we traveled together through the pass. Though we never spoke of it, all of us were terrified, watching and listening for the Killers in the dark. I stayed so close to my mom I was like a giant barnacle on her flank.

The next morning, in the light, we found exactly what we feared most— Killers in the pass! They were busy terrifying a sea lion colony and didn't notice us. The sea lions were barking a warning to each other. One of them swam up to me and barked, "Code black! Code black! Everyone out of the pool!"

FAST FACTS
Isanotski Strait, also known as False Pass, near Unimak Island, Alaska, is known for killer whale attacks on gray whales.

We tried to get away without being seen and traveled farther along the pass before spotting more Killers. They had surrounded a gray whale calf. The calf looked to be my age.

One of the Whale Killers had the calf's flipper in its mouth and was trying to pull it under water. My stomach wrenched.

The young gray whale's mother was waging war with more Killers nearby. One, a big male, was all white and really scary! The mother was desperately trying to return to her youngster. Close to the action were two terrified Pacific white-sided dolphins, fleeing toward a nearby kelp bed where they could hide. We picked up our pace, until we were swimming as fast as a gray whale can swim, at least with a calf like me slowing things down. When we were at a safe distance from them, I asked my mother what she thought would happen to the calf.

"That calf doesn't have a chance, not a chance," she told me.

"Can't we do something?" I pleaded, "Shouldn't we help them?"

"It is my job to keep you safe, not bring you into danger," she declared.

"That's right," said the two other gray whale mothers traveling with us.

"What if it was us back there?" I asked. "What if it was me who had his flipper being bitten by those whales? What about what you taught me, Mom? What you learned when the knowledge was given about helping others? What if that old dolphin had made a different choice? We might not be here now!"

"Stop it! You are my responsibility!" My mom was almost in tears. After a long pause she said, "You are right, my precious little calf. We must make the right choice here, so I am going to go back and help that poor whale. You stay here with them!" She motioned toward the two whale moms. "May the Creator of all things have mercy on us all!"

Before I could even try to change her mind about being left behind, I heard the two other moms say, "Sorry, count us out! We are leaving! It is way too dangerous in this place!"

They left quickly without even saying goodbye.

Mom understood their reasons. "Maybe those dolphins back there know that danger sound," she explained. "I was going to go back to see if they could help. Now I don't know what to do. This wouldn't have even been a choice in the days before our eyes were opened."

"Let's do it, Mom! Let's do it!" I cried as I watched her impatiently swim in a tight circle, unsure if she really wanted to take the risk. "Those Killers are pretty busy. They probably will not even notice us," she said more to herself than to me. "Okay, you stay right next to me. We'll go in real close to shore where it's calm and where those dolphins are hiding in the kelp."

We turned and swam slowly and carefully back, toward the dolphins and closer to our greatest fear. We got in real tight to shore and quietly slipped into the kelp near the white-sided dolphins. They looked like terrified miniature Whale Killers, black and white and scared all over. We were close enough to be seen by the Killers (if we were on the surface), but they were too busy maiming and attacking to notice us. The dolphins relaxed once they got a good look at us and saw we weren't Killers.

My mom asked in a nervous whisper: "Do either of you know how to make the Killers' danger call?" The dolphins were literally paralyzed with fear, since Whale Killers have been eating dolphins for generations too.

"Well?" my mom angrily whispered to the do-nothing duo.

"Ye-yes," one of them stuttered, "b-but I have never done it."

"Well just do it now! Before those killers finish off that calf and come looking for you! *Now!*" My mom whispered angrily right in the dolphin's face.

The dolphin was afraid of being discovered by the Killers if he didn't make the sound right, but my mom was seven times his size and getting madder by the second.

"Do it, Philly," said his friend.

"Shut up, Herb! I don't need any more pressure here."

He went to the bottom, closed his eyes and concentrated like we had once seen that old dolphin do.

That terrible, beautiful, high-pitched scream filled the ocean all around us with its sound. We waited silently for what seemed like forever, until I could not hold my breath another second! We surfaced and carefully scanned the horizon. We didn't see any sign of the Whale Killers, or the mom and calf. Everyone was gone. We waited a while to be sure they weren't under water. Then we said goodbye to Philly and Herb and they took off.

We didn't stop again until we finished making it through that awful pass and into The Coldest Place.

In The Coldest Place, we often saw Caretakers setting whale traps, what you call fishing nets, so we were constantly looking out for them. It was even more frightening at night when we couldn't see them.

We had many days and nights with strong winds and rough seas in The Coldest Place, but under the water it was usually surprisingly calm.

Shortly after we made it through The Pass, a male person with a long pole came after me. I decided instantly that he was one of the hunters my mom had warned me about, so I immediately dove down to get away from him, and to find my mom.

But just as I was getting deep, another whale called down to me, "Don't be afraid!" the whale shouted, "He's a teacher and a good Caretaker who's helped many of us! His name is Ed."

So I surfaced and slowed down, and the man in the red jacket, Ed, came right up next to me. I was scared, really scared! But I wanted and needed to trust him. He reached out with the long pole and cut the rope, on one side, that sliced into my mouth and I was feeling a lot better.

Just then my mom surfaced, saw the pole and another boat coming, and ordered me to leave immediately! I tried to explain what the other whale had told me, but her eyes let me know her fear. I had to go with her now, or she would leave me behind. So we dove down quickly and left the area. Mom usually knew best. There were many dangers she saw that I didn't. But I believe that this time she was wrong not to trust these Caretakers and make me swim away.

After that, Mom spent most of her days feeding. I watched her dive down, suck mud from the bottom into her mouth, then push the mud and sediment out through the baleen plates in her mouth, using them as a filter. She would end up with lots of little amphipods in her mouth, which she then swallowed whole. It was strange to see her eat so much because Mom had rarely eaten anything, until the last few weeks.

FAST FACTS

Gray whales normally don't need to dive any deeper than about 100 ft. (30 meters) but they can dive to about 395 ft. (120 meters). Their hearts, which weigh about 287 pounds, normally beat at a rate of 8-10 beats a minute but slow to 4-5 beats during a deep dive. Gray whales can store a lot more oxygen in their muscles than we can: Gray whales 41%, Humans 13%.

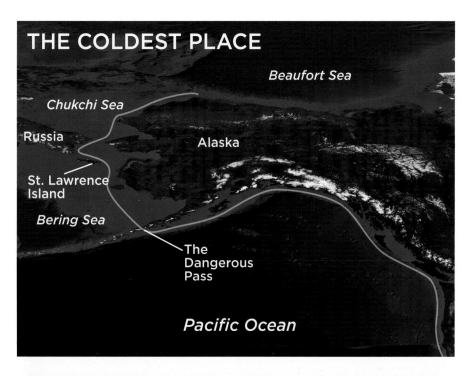

THE COLDEST PLACE

Beaufort Sea

Chukchi Sea

Russia

Alaska

St. Lawrence
Island

Bering Sea

The
Dangerous
Pass

Pacific Ocean

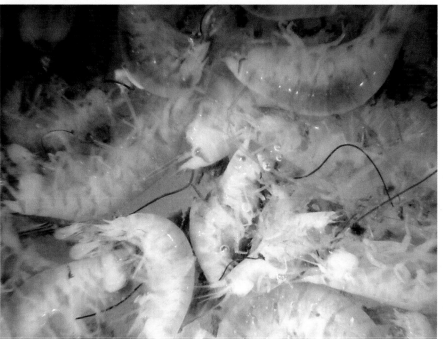

I decided to try to copy her. She thought that was a great idea and said, "Yes, I think it's time for you to begin feeding yourself."

Starting in The Lagoon, Mom had showed me how to suck mud from the bottom even though there was nothing there to eat. Now these amphipods were actually kind of tasty, but I still preferred Mom's milk to the amphipods.

These were good days for both of us. Day after day, Mom and I ate and I explored. And the next day, I played and we ate some more. The days were very long, and it hardly ever got dark.

FAST FACTS
Feeding grounds in the Bering and Chukchi seas are normally shallow: 165-225 ft /50-68 meters.

One day I saw a couple of boats heading our way. They held Caretakers with long poles with ropes and buoys attached, just like the male person, Ed, who helped me before. I decided not to tell Mom and have her ruin it by making me run away. I was really scared! Everything in me wanted to swim away quickly! But I waited on the surface for the boats to get next to me. This time I was going to get free! They drifted closer and closer, and I jumped for joy. But these Caretakers were not trying to help me after all. One of them threw one of those long poles at me and I heard an awful thud and felt a sharp electrifying pain, more painful than anything I've ever known. It turned out to be a harpoon! After the harpoon hit me it bounced off my back, but part of it stuck in me. There was a rope attached with a big red buoy, and it slowed me way down. Then another struck, delivering the same intense pain to another area of my back. These were the aboriginal hunters my mom had warned me about, and I was in serious trouble!

They took out these long sticks that made loud popping noises. Something stung my back several times. I was bleeding.

Mom surfaced between me and the boats to protect me. We heard more loud explosions and then Mom got stung too.

We both dove underwater. I strained and struggled to go as fast and as deep as I could. We sank together beneath the water. Those two air-filled buoys were trying to pull me back to the surface. All of a sudden I felt something rip loose. One of the buoys, with a harpoon attached, shot to the surface. It was easier to swim after that, so I plunged deeper until I felt the other harpoon tear loose. I turned to see it dolphining toward the surface. We got as far away from that place as fast as we could. And as we swam, I thought about what my mom had told me back in The Lagoon, and right there and then I promised myself, and her, that I would never ever trust another Caretaker again.

FAST FACTS

From 2008 to 2012, up to 140 gray whales could be legally hunted every year in Russian waters. More on this in Grown Up Stuff at the end of this book.

When I looked at my mom I couldn't believe my eyes. She was bleeding from several different places where the stings hit her. She looked awful. I guess we both did, and I thought for sure she was not going to make it.

"I'm okay," she exclaimed, "most of the stings just nicked me."

The same was true for me, thankfully—although we both did have a couple of deep wounds. My mom then did something really surprising, she told me a joke. "Two Caretakers were sitting in a kayak," she said, "and they were very cold. To keep warm, they lit a fire in the craft, but the craft caught fire and sank. They should have understood," she explained, "you can't have your kayak and heat it, too!"

My mom, unlike my Uncle Mike, hardly ever told a joke, and when she did it was usually for a good reason. I think she was trying to explain the foolishness of Caretakers—how they support themselves by taking other Caretakers out to see us, like your dad does, Arielle, but then they kill us with harpoons and fishing traps. They sometimes even eat us, like the Whale Killers.

"Lily, not all Caretakers want to kill whales," explained Arielle. "Most of us are like the killer whales who eat fish. We don't want to hurt you!"

"So you say," said a skeptical Lily. She then continued with her story:

Anyway, there were lots of amphipods everywhere on the bottom in that area and lots of whales feeding all around us. One day when I was down at the bottom sucking mud, a whale swam up from behind me, and without even saying hello, he asked, "What did one whale's barnacle say to another whale's barnacle? Nothing," he said, answering his own question, "barnacles can't talk!"

No one could tell a bad joke like my Uncle Mike, who shook the ocean with his laughter.

Mom and I were really happy to see good old Uncle Mike. He hung out with us for several days, feeding and telling stories as we continued to make our way into colder and colder water. That first night we spent hours and hours talking, mostly about what had happened since we had last seen each other. Uncle Mike was pretty quiet when I told him about all that I had been through. Then after I finished talking, he gave me the names of several whales who didn't make it back to The Lagoon last season. Some of them were caught in nets, others were taken by Killers, and some just disappeared. The next day while my mom was down feeding, Uncle Mike told me a story that my mom had never told me.

"You see this area here?" Uncle Mike began. "It used to completely ice over every fall, though it hasn't for several years. Anyway, one year it iced over so fast that your great-grandmother and two of her friends got caught in a hole in the ice. Several Caretakers helped free her. It took them a long time, and they used some huge ships to make a way for her to escape the ice. Listen, your mom doesn't trust Caretakers," Uncle Mike lowered his voice,

"but just between you and me, humans are not all bad. In fact, some of the Caretakers who helped your great-grandmother were even known to hunt and kill bowhead whales before they helped her."

Uncle Mike stayed with us for several days, till we lost track of him as we continued foraging along the coast.

We spotted a group of beluga whales one day. They were nearly as white as the ice and talked all the time—yak-yak-yak. They are even worse than the common dolphins!

We spotted some weird-looking narwhals. My mom explained to me that the males have a tooth that pokes out of their mouth like a long, bony, pointed stick. I almost got accidentally jabbed by one when he swam a little too close. We saw hundreds of comical looking walruses too.

As the days passed into weeks, Mom gave me less and less milk, until I was mostly just feeding on amphipods.

We had to be careful where we surfaced because sometimes there was ice above us.

By this time, most of our wounds had healed over.

Then early one morning, a long time after being attacked by the hunters, Mom breached again. It was the first time she had jumped out of the water since the hunter's stings had wounded her. I was so happy to see her feeling better. When she leaped into the air, I noticed all the scratches on her skin from the killer whales and all of her wounds, and I thought about how much we had been through together. We whales call our scars "the tracks of our tears." Every whale has a story for every scar.

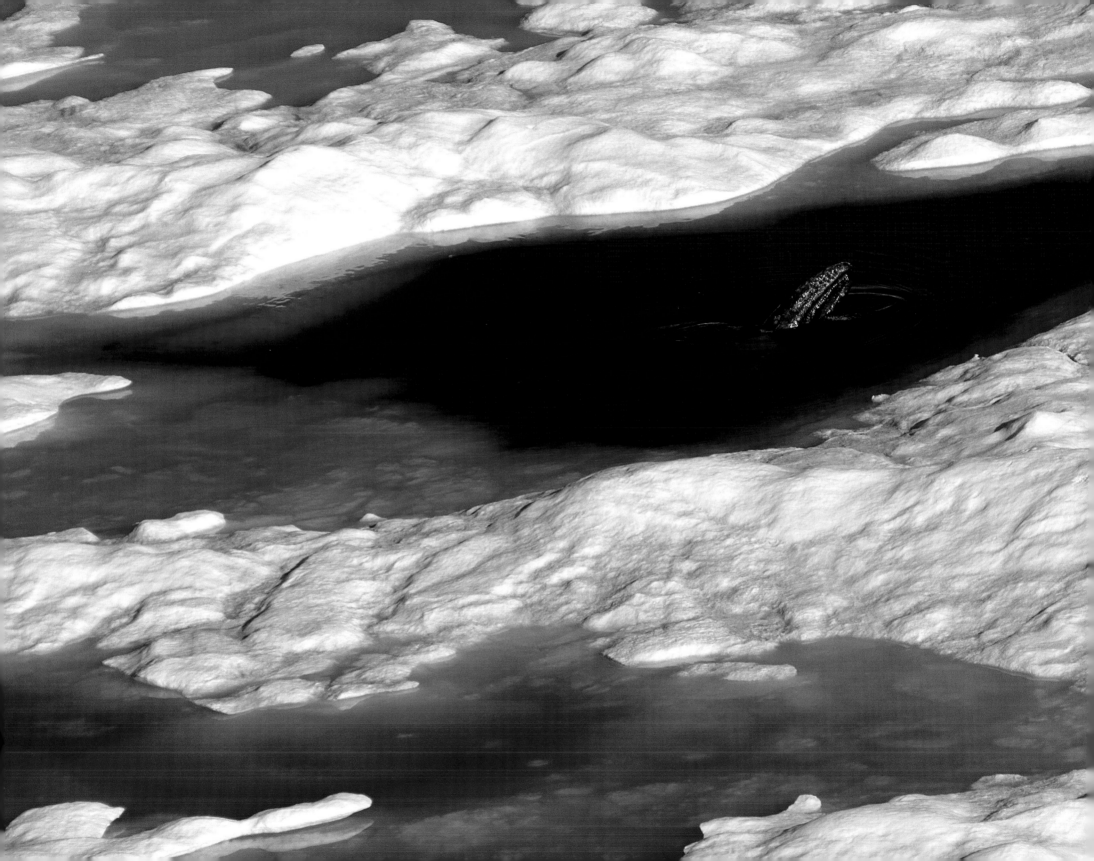

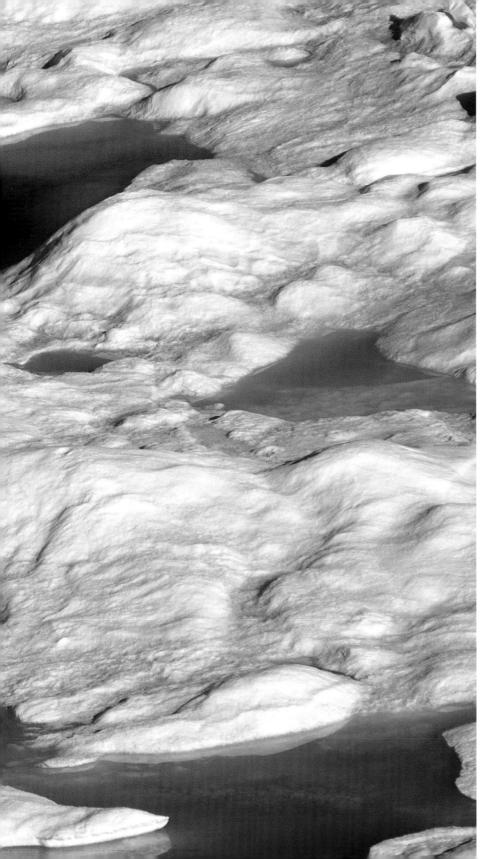

As we continued foraging, the ice became bigger and thicker. One time when I surfaced, I found myself surrounded by ice like my grandmother! And my mom, who had been feeding with me, was nowhere to be found! I nervously waited on the surface. I looked and looked, all around. I screamed out, "Mom!" on the surface and underwater, as loud as I could, but I was alone. In fact, I was more alone than any creature on earth. I was afraid to move in any direction, fearing it would take me farther from her. I might have stayed there in that spot forever, paralyzed with fear, if it had not been for . . .

. . . the polar bear.

He called out to me, "Hey, whale, come here. I want to tell you some-thing."

"What is it?" I asked.

"Come a little closer. I don't want anyone else to hear."

Well, believe me, there was no one else around for at least a day's swim, so naturally I was a little suspicious. I moved as close to his ice floe as I dared.

The bear bent down toward me in the water and said, "Listen, whale. There is not a lot of food for me here, and, well, if you come just a little closer I will tell you something."

"I am close enough, bear!" I declared, "What do you want?"

"Well, I was wondering, have you seen any seals or beluga whales or anything edible around here?"

"No, I'm sorry, I haven't. Even if I had, I would not tell you!"

"Well, that's not very friendly. I'm hungry and you could help me," the bear growled angrily.

"Well, I'm sorry you're hungry but I . . . "

"So what are you doing in this hole?" he interrupted.

"I am trying to find my mom. We got separated."

"Oh, really," he said in a sympathetic voice, "Does she look like you only bigger?"

"Yes!"

"Oh, I know where she is."

"Where?" I begged, "Where?"

"It's a little hard to explain, but if you come closer, I will draw you a map in the ice."

I looked at the bear, and I noticed the bear

was salivating with a real faraway look on his face, like he was remembering something.

"I am so hungry I could eat a bear," wailed the bear.

"Or a whale," I said moving farther away.

"Whale, if you could read my thoughts, you would know my true intentions."

"Sorry, bear, but my mom told me to stay away from bears."

I knew exactly what that bear was thinking: "Hey, I wonder if gray whales taste as good as bowhead whales do?"

So I dove down and left that hole behind. Any direction was better than staying there with the bear. Anyway, my mom had said just that morning that it was about time to start heading back toward The Lagoon. So after a long day with the bear, and no sign of Mom, I decided to do what she would do—I started heading back.

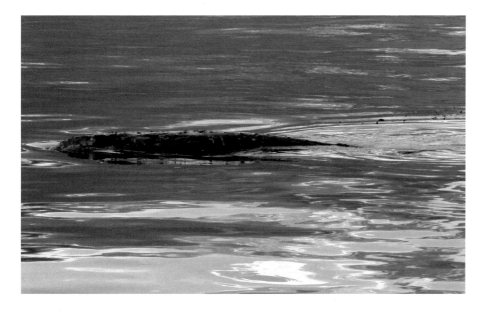

Fortunately, I was able to find enough breathing holes in the ice to get out of there.

After two days of nothing but ice, it finally began to thin out. In a few more days, I was back out in the open ocean again.

When I first lost my mom, I was terrified. Then after a few days something inside told me it was going to be all right. My mom had stayed with me longer than she should have, because of the net. Now it was time for me to be on my own.

I felt sort of ready for the journey back to The Lagoon. I also felt certain that I would meet up with my mom again there.

But one night I was feeling very alone again when I saw the great lights overhead. I stopped swimming and stared in awe at the lights in the sky above me. The moment I saw this green glow my loneliness vanished. It was His glory. As I stayed still and looked and listened, I remembered the first time that my mom and I had seen these strange lights and every word she had said: "Our world has always had colors," she explained, "but there was a time when we just didn't notice them. Now when we witness the great lights in the sky over The Coldest Place, or a setting sun, it is much more than just the end of the day...it is something to behold."

CHAPTER SEVEN

A Long Way to the Lagoon

As I revisited the places that Mom and I had passed through, it felt like she was still with me. I was scared, hopeful and excited about the journey ahead; but it was a long way to The Lagoon. With the netting digging into me, I still couldn't travel very fast.

Eventually, I made my way to The Dangerous Pass. My mom had told me that there shouldn't be as many Whale Killers waiting for us on the return trip to The Lagoon. Still, I waited outside the pass and went through with another whale, just in case. The weather was much nicer this time, and we made it through the pass without any problems. Afterwards I noticed that the other whale had some bad scars on him that looked like teeth marks. Normally, we gray whales don't talk much to strangers, but I decided to ask about them.

"Yeah," he told me, "My mom and I got ambushed in The Pass. A Killer was dragging me around by my flipper, and I was saying my prayers, when we heard the strangest sound, then every one of those Killers just took off!"

"Was one of the Killers all white?" I asked.

"Yes!"

I couldn't believe my ears. This was the young whale we had saved. I explained to him the whole story, going back to the old dolphin who saved my mom and I.

My fellow traveler froze and stared at me in disbelief. "It was you?"

"Yes! Well, it was the dolphin who made the sound. But my mom and I stayed, and, well, I guess it was actually my idea to help you!" I bragged.

He swam next to me and rubbed himself up against me. I guess it's what you would call a whale hug. He thanked me over and over again for saving his life, and promised to stay with me all the way to The Lagoon. He vowed to help other whales in trouble if he ever ran across any. At just that moment, right after I had told him the story, we heard a sound. It was faint at first then it became clearly recognizable—a terrible, beautiful sound. We both recognized the danger sound coming from straight ahead of us. Since we were only a few feet under the water, we surfaced to see what it was. To my absolute horror a huge ship was bearing down on us. It was so close it seemed impossible for us to get out of the way without being run over. We both dove without a word and swam for our lives.

The bow of the ship ripped through the water inches from my flukes! I could feel a great wave of water push me away with a mighty force behind it! Two white-sided dolphins were bow riding on the front of the ship. "There's another gray whale up ahead, Philly—make the sound!" Herb cried. We heard the danger sound again. As our old friends Philly and Herb passed us they laughed. They were having the time of their lives, catching a free "surf" ride on the front of this massive ship and warning whales that crossed paths with them.

That was a close call for both of us, but it wasn't the first time for me or the last close encounter we had together. Two other ships nearly ran us over during the time that my new best friend, "Stony," was traveling with me. We stayed together day and night from the full moon to no moon. Then one dark night during a storm, we lost track of each other.

So I continued on my own, stopping to eat wherever I found amphipods or herring eggs or anything else edible that I could catch, like krill or shrimp. As I made my way down the coast, I tried to stick real close to shore so I wouldn't get lost.

I kept watching out for nets, but sometimes they were nearly impossible to avoid.

One afternoon I heard a little voice.

"Hey, Stinky, can you give me a flipper? Over here, I am caught in this stupid net."

"Are you talking to me?" I asked the entangled sea otter.

"Yeah," he squeaked, "I remember you and your mom passed gas through here a while back. You're easy to recognize with the net décor on your flukes and all. Now look at me. I've got the same outfit. How 'bout some help?"

"What am I supposed to do?" I asked, "I can't even get the net that's on me off."

"There's got to be a way. Maybe you can have a look and tell me which way to thrash and turn to untangle myself? I keep making it worse."

I gave it a try, and what do you know—after about an hour he was free.

"Well how 'bout if I return the favor?" he asked me.

"Sure, you can try," I replied.

"Let me see . . ." He looked my net over. "Let me chew on this awhile and see what I can do."

And that is exactly what he did. He chewed on it until sunset. He actually got some of the rope and netting off before he broke a tooth and was in so much pain he had to stop.

"Sorry, whale, gotta go and find my buddies."

He left, and then I was alone again.

I continued my long, slow slog down the coast. This time I knew how far I had to go, and it only made it worse every flip of my flukes!

I then spotted something that made my head swim like I was doing a deep dive and made my stomach feel like it did the time I accidentally swallowed a plastic bag, Whale Killers! "Not again!" I thought. I looked around for local dolphins to make that danger sound. "None around!"

One of the Killers swam straight for me. I turned and tried to escape, swimming as fast as I could, but he quickly overtook me. I didn't dare turn around. I could see his shadow just above me. I tightened my muscles and waited for the pain that his bite would soon bring.

"Hey wait up!" said the Killer, in a friendly voice. My terror broke open and spilled out enough joy to fill the entire ocean. It was Buddy! "Surprised to see me?" he asked as he came alongside.

"Definitely," I said, catching my breath. Buddy continued, "I came here and joined up with these Fisheaters. It took me awhile to get in. Listen, I am the first Whale Killer ever to be let into a Fisheater pod in the entire natural history of the world! They not only accept me for who I am, but I will never, ever have to kill a whale again! Even though you guys do taste better than salmon," he laughed. "Isn't that great?"

I wanted to tell Buddy how happy I was, but the words wouldn't come out. Only tears that instantly washed away underwater expressed my deepest affections for this former Whale Killer. He introduced me to his podmates,

and they all followed along next to me. Buddy even caught a few salmon, tore them up a bit and then he spit them out for me to eat. He was a true friend. I had to keep moving and the pod followed along with me. They even tried chewing the net off like the sea otter. Eventually they got some of it off, but their teeth just weren't suited to the job, and they all hurt themselves trying. Eventually, after a few days, we had to go our separate ways.

"I'll see you next season on your way back to The Coldest Place!" Buddy said with a hopeful, upbeat tone.

I wasn't so sure about that.

As I moved further down the coast, food became scarcer, and what was available was harder for me to catch. It took so much energy to swim. I was in a lot of pain from the net, which continued to saw deeper into me whenever I moved my tail flukes up and down to swim. After a while, I used up what was left of my reserves, and every day that passed I became hungrier and weaker. I was slowly starving to death. I tried not to think about how far I had to go, or how I would ever make it back to The Coldest Place. I just took it minute by minute. I set only short goals for myself, saying I just need to make it to that rock up ahead, or that kelp bed up ahead, or whatever. I tried not to think about food, or the pain in my peduncle and flukes from the netting.

Eventually I made my way to the Deep Canyon. I didn't bother to wait for any whales to catch me before crossing because, as far as I could tell, there were no other whales left behind me. They all had passed me. I felt certain that I was now the last gray whale coming down the coast. The sun was getting hotter, and I started seeing more Caretakers on the beach. Most of the time they didn't even notice me. I felt like I was invisible. They were so close. I wanted so much for one of them to swim out and assist me with their helpful arms and hands. It would be so easy for them to remove this net, and my constant companion—pain! But I wasn't about to trust any of them, ever again.

Every time I spotted gray whales heading up the coast, I would think about how they had just spent months in the lagoons—playing, resting, enjoying life, enjoying each others' company, reuniting with family—and how they were on their way back now to The Coldest Place where there was so much food. The more I thought about these whales, the more I began to feel utterly and completely alone and without hope.

In the pit of my despair, I decided to shift my hope to the eternal life that my mom had told me about. She had learned that the Creator, who does not lie, promised it before the beginning of time. I quit swimming, drifted into a calm cove, and slept all that night and all the next day. I was in no hurry. Where I was going now, I would not have to swim to get there.

In the morning I awoke from my half sleep to a sound, a noise like another whale, in the distance. I opened my eyes. I could barely make out a whale swimming toward me in the murky blue underwater fog. I heard a faint, familiar voice, "How do you keep a niece in suspense for a day?"

Was I imagining things? I didn't care if I was. "Uncle Mike!" I screamed as I moved toward the shadowy figure of Uncle Mike.

"I'll tell you tomorrow," he said, answering his own riddle. He laughed and when he rubbed up against me, I knew for sure that Uncle Mike was real.

"You don't look so good," he said. "You need to come with me, right now, back to The Coldest Place and get some food in you."

"I can't make it that far," I replied. "I just want to see my mother one more time."

"Your mom? She is still waiting at The Lagoon. Just about everyone else already left, but she stayed and is looking for you. Listen, I'll go with you there." Uncle Mike casually offered, as if it was no big deal. But it was a big deal. It was a very big deal. I knew if he stayed with me, Uncle Mike could easily run out of reserves and die, too.

"No," I said. "You have to keep going."

He looked at me for a long time. Then I knew he understood.

Uncle Mike stayed with me till the sun was straight overhead. He told me about all the crazy stuff that had happened in The Lagoon while he was there: who did what and where, who was courting who, and so on. We both released the gift of laughter, and I felt better inside, better than I had in a long time. Usually goodbyes were easy for us whales because we keep running into each other on our migrations, but this was the hardest goodbye ever. We both understood that it would

be the last time in this world that we would ever see each other. We both knew I was too weak to make it to The Lagoon, never mind all the way back to The Coldest Place.

Uncle Mike told me a joke, said a quick goodbye, then he swam away without looking back. Both of us released the gift of tears. That is one gift I wish we had never been given.

I got a surge of energy the morning after Uncle Mike left, and I began swimming down the coast again, if you could call it swimming. I was barely moving. I checked out every gray whale that I passed along the way in the hopes of finding my mother. I just wanted to see her one more time. By the time I was out in front of your harbor, I was completely broken, finished. I couldn't even raise my flukes anymore. I had no more hopes of finding my mother, or of making it to The Lagoon, or of making it anywhere.

I decided to break my promise never to trust the Caretakers outside of The Lagoon, and I entered the harbor. I headed to the blue building in the harbor that you had told my mom about so long ago, so that the Caretakers there could help me . . . or they could kill me. And I waited to see what they would do.

CHAPTER EIGHT

The Disentanglement

"That's my story," Lily concluded.

"Wow, that is the most amazing story I have ever heard in my entire life!" Arielle declared, and she meant it. "Don't worry, Lily. While you were talking, my dad and his friend Dean, who rescues sea lions and stuff, spotted that net on you. They saw the netting, Lily! They called Mr. Joe at the Natural Fish Service (National Marine Fisheries Service). He's the boss when it comes to helping the whales, and he said that if you are still here tomorrow, they will get that net off you! Isn't that great?"

"Well, that would be a good thing. I really wish my mom were here," Lily said wearily. "We went through so much together. I miss her." Lily tried to put her mom out of her thoughts and be thankful. "Well, tomorrow it is," she said to herself. "They will bring their long pole with a knife to cut the rope or a harpoon to do me in," she said weakly. "Either way, I will be waiting."

Lily sounded braver than she actually felt inside. Inside she was terrified.

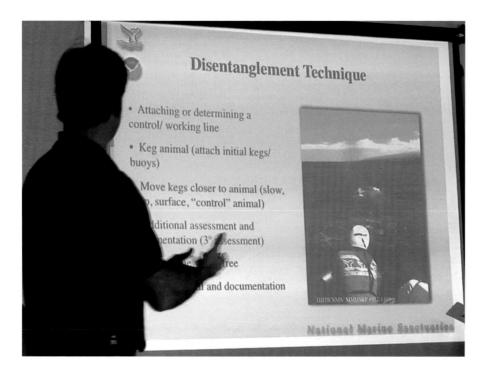

The next day Lily was waiting, right in front of the very building where two years earlier Capt. Dave, Dean and others were trained to do disentanglements by NOAA (National Oceanic and Atmospheric Administration)—the blue building.

On the way to help Lily, Capt. Dave drove to the harbor with his wife, Gisele, and Arielle. Arielle had some questions for her father. Now that Lily had shared her life story with her, Arielle felt responsible for Lily's safety. She wanted to do all she could to help.

"Dad, I know Lily is scared. What if she tries to run away from you or accidentally hurts you? Can't you let me go with you, so I can talk to her?"

"I can't, Honey. It's too dangerous," her father explained for the third time.

"But, Dad, I know you tried to help a whale before and you couldn't," Arielle reasoned. "Are you sure you can get that net off her?"

"You mean that humpback whale two years ago?"

"Yes."

"That was different, Little One. Two years ago we didn't have the proper tools or the training. Orange County didn't even have a whale rescue group back then, so I organized one and I convinced Mr. Joe to send someone to train us. We are much more ready now than we were for that last poor whale."

"How are you going to get that net off? What kind of stuff did they teach you, Dad, that will help Lily?"

"Well," her dad continued, "our teacher was a guy named Ed Lyman who works with NOAA. He showed everyone how to get netting and fishing gear off a whale, and we even practiced with the tools. Ed normally works in Hawaii and Alaska disentangling whales."

"Dad, I think Mr. Ed might be the good Caretaker that Lily told me she met in Alaska! He tried to help her there!" Arielle exclaimed.

"Well, it's possible," her dad replied, not realizing that Arielle was right.

"Dad, when you get in the water with her, tell her about Mr. Ed!"

"We won't be getting in the water, Arielle. One of the things we learned from Mr. Ed is to never go in the water with a whale because it is very dangerous. There could be netting hanging off the whale, and a rescuer could get tangled in it and drown. Even though whales are normally very gentle, you never know what a whale might do when you start pulling on that netting. It might even panic and accidentally hurt you because it is frightened.

"So instead of going into the water, he showed us how to use a long pole that comes in five-foot sections, so it can be lengthened. We can attach special hooks and knives to the end of it to help remove the netting and rope from a whale. We learned a lot, Arielle; hopefully Lily will cooperate."

As Captain Dave made his way to the dock, other team members who had been trained began to arrive.

There were also a few other highly skilled people, like a rescue diver, who had not been through disentanglement training. They were asked by Capt. Dave and Dean to stand by, in case someone accidentally fell in and was hurt.

Mr. Joe from NMFS put the folks from Sea World in charge of the Orange County group because they had more experience rescuing whales. Once Eric and Jody from Sea World arrived, the first boat pulled away, with Capt. Dave, Dean, Eric, and Dana on Dana's boat.

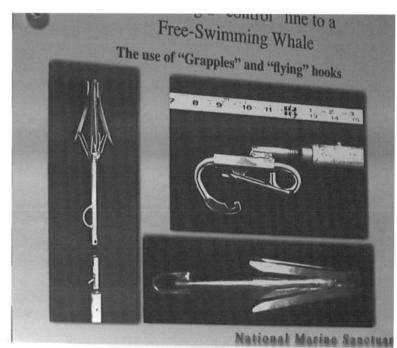

Free-Swimming Whale
The use of "Grapples" and "flying" hooks

National Marine Sanctuary

Arielle stayed on shore with her best friend, Josten. They would be part of the shore-side team, listening on the radio to all the interaction between the two boats, ready to run and help or get other supplies or tools that might be needed. There were three news helicopters hovering overhead.

Lots of people came to the harbor to see Lily get help. Many of them had come every day to see her in the harbor, and as news spread about her upcoming rescue, they lined up all around the shore to watch.

Arielle called out to Lily from shore, "I wish I could be near you, so you would have someone to talk to. But I have to stay here!"

Then she picked up a feather she found and put it in her pocket to give to Lily later as a reminder of their friendship. As she thought about giving Lily the feather, Arielle suddenly realized that Lily did not have any way to keep a feather or a home to put it in. She didn't even have any pockets. In fact, Lily had no possessions of any kind. For the first time, Arielle wondered what it was really like to be a whale, like Lily. She shouted one more time to her friend. "Don't worry, Lily. Everything's going to be okay!"

"I trust you, Arielle," Lily replied in a raspy, weak voice, but Arielle was too far away to hear her.

On the rescue boat the first thing Capt. Dave and the team did was observe Lily to see how she would react to them getting close to her and to determine where the netting was on her. They found she had netting wrapped around her tail flukes and her peduncle area (stock of her tail flukes). She also had a rope that was hard to see; it stretched from one side of her mouth to her tail flukes.

When the team saw Lily up close, she looked very emaciated. They talked about it and were worried that she seemed very weak. Some even thought that she wouldn't make it. The team knew that getting the net off her would increase her odds of survival, so they decided to begin the disentanglement.

Whenever Capt. Dave wasn't needed for something else, he tried to take as many photos and as much video as possible. The video would help the team train for any future whale rescues. His footage and photos could also be used later to teach others about the problem of whales getting tangled in nets and, hence, raise awareness of the problem and save more whales and dolphins from Lily's fate.

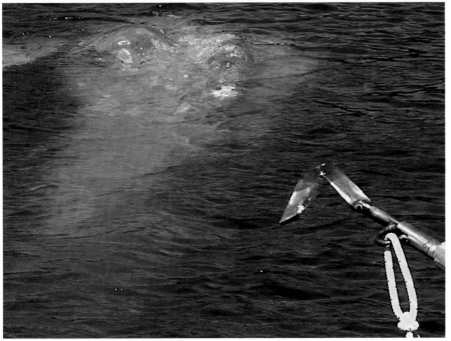

When Lily first saw the Caretakers, she noticed they had a long pole with a rope and a big orange buoy attached to it, just like the hunters in The Coldest Place. She wanted to understand what the Caretakers were saying, but she could only understand Arielle. Frightened, Lily got a surge of adrenaline.

"It's a trick!" she thought. "I'll swim away!" Then she remembered she had asked for help. "Calm down," she told herself. "Calm down!"

Using their specially designed long pole and a special hook, they clipped a 50-foot long rope with a big red buoy to the netting near Lily's tail flukes.

Lily felt them attach something to the net. It didn't hurt, but it pulled at her and slowed her down.

"Why are they doing this? They're trying to drown me! I'm going to thrash around and knock it off," she thought.

Getting the control line on was an important first step to avoid losing Lily in case she bolted. With it they could hold on to the rope, and Lily would pull them along with her wherever she went. In the whaling days, this was called a Nantucket sleigh ride. They hoped Lily wouldn't be taking them on any wild rides.

Once this line was attached, everyone needed to be completely committed to finishing the job, because the control line would initially make things harder for her. Also, if Lily started swimming too fast, they could attach more buoys to slow her down.

Using the control line, the team pulled themselves right up next to Lily.

Then using the pole, they attached a jam knife to the netting, and then another.

"Hey, watch out with that!" Lily exclaimed fearfully, exhaling an enormous breath, as their knife brushed her skin. But no one understood her.

Eric and Capt. Dave agreed that Lily could have used a breath mint.

Lily thought their boat could have used a fish mint.

Lily didn't need to worry because the V-shaped jam knives have a cutting edge on the inside of the V so that they won't cut into her. These knives also have a long rope and a buoy attached to them.

Once attached to the netting, they released the knife from the pole. As Lily slowly swam through the water, she discovered she was now dragging another big orange floating ball. Normally as the ball moves through the water, there would be considerable pressure pulling on the jam knife. This would cause the knife to shake back and forth, cutting through the netting and causing it to drop off. This is what it was designed to do.

Dragging the orange ball through the water reminded Lily of when the hunters had a buoy attached to the harpoon they had stuck into her—except this time it didn't hurt.

"Why are you attaching things to me?" Lily shouted, though no one understood her sounds. "You are supposed to be helping me!" she cried.

Lily felt a panic rise in her she could not control. She began swimming as fast as she could, away from the team. Arielle grabbed the radio from her mom and spoke. Lily could hear Arielle's voice over the handheld radio, "Don't run away, Lily! Listen, they are trying to help you!" Arielle then explained how the tools worked. Lily listened, but after all she had been through, she couldn't fully trust the disentanglement team—or anyone else except Arielle— and *that* she was only able to do moment to moment.

Lily stopped swimming away.

After she stopped, the team recognized that Lily was not able to move fast enough for the knives to cut through the netting. So they decided to try something different, something a little riskier.

They began pulling hard on the ropes attached to the knives in the hope that the knives would cut through the netting. Lily could feel them tugging on her tail flukes.

Arielle called out to Lily, "Lily, it's okay. You can trust them. They are trying to help you."

Lily relaxed her whole body.

Instead of fighting them, Lily just let go. The team members pulled on the ropes attached to the jam knives, but they did not cut through the net; instead, they actually pulled Lily's tail flukes up to the surface, which surprised everyone!

Then they were able to cut the netting and the rope off by hand. Dana, who had been doing a great job handling the boat and keeping people from poking it with sharp objects, handed Eric a knife.

They had to be very careful working so close to Lily's powerful tail flukes. Lily had no idea how strong she was, even in her weakened state. Although Lily was very gentle, she would occasionally swim slowly away from them, and when she did, they had to let go of the ropes quickly, or she could pull them in.

> **FAST FACTS**
>
> Lily was a young 26-foot gray whale, but she looked really old because she had lots of yellowish whale lice on her. When a whale has lots of injuries, these lice attach themselves around the dead skin, which is what they eat.

And that's exactly what happened! Lily got scared and pulled away. Capt. Dave and Eric released their grip, but Dean was so fully committed to helping Lily, he wasn't able to let go fast enough. He plunged into the water with Lily, unwillingly breaking the rule not to get in the water.

"Sorry, Caretaker, I didn't mean to pull you in." Lily felt bad that she was so scared.

Eric and Capt. Dave helped Dean back into the boat.

Everyone was watching Lily and hoping she would soon be free.

There were so many whale lice on Lily that they were actually crawling onto the hands of the rescue team while they were working. Capt. Dave put some in a cup to show Arielle later on.

After Dean got pulled in, Eric, being a good team leader, decided to rotate team members to give others an opportunity to help Lily. So Capt. Dave asked Tom to take his place on the lead boat, and Eric asked Jody to replace Dean. However, because Capt. Tom knew how much Barry wanted to get his hands on that netting, he made the unselfish choice to give up this rare opportunity and let Barry take his place.

With Barry and Jody on the lead boat, the team finished cutting off what they hoped to be the last of the netting.

FAST FACTS

Female whale lice have a marsupium, or pouch, that holds their unhatched eggs, and also the baby whale lice after they hatch. This assures the baby lice will be on the whale's skin once they are able to crawl away. Whale lice feed on a whale's dead skin. Baby gray whales most likely get their lice from physical contact with their mother. One variety of whale lice, *Cyamus scammoni*, can grow to 1.5 inches and are so prevalent that on the skin of a single gray whale over 100,000 of them were once found.

The crowd on shore cheered as they saw Barry lift the netting into the air. Arielle, Josten, Mark, and Gisele jumped up and down for joy, along with the entire team on both boats. In less than four hours since the effort had started, Lily was free from the nets at last!

No one had been hurt, including Lily, and it had all been done in the calm of the peaceful harbor waters instead of out in the open sea where most disentanglements take place. Members of the team marveled at how Lily had just happened to come to the quiet harbor waters, to the very blue building where they had been trained two years before she had arrived. Some people watching from shore wondered out loud if Lily might have actually come into the harbor looking for help.

During the disentanglement, Lily had been, ever so slowly, making her way toward the harbor entrance. Her movements were so sluggish that it was obvious to most of the team members that she was very weak. She stopped near the entrance.

Lily had thousands of miles to travel to The Coldest Place. She knew her chances were very slim of making it, but after so many people had worked so hard to help, she had to at least try. As she left the harbor, Lily called out to Arielle, the team, and all the people watching, "Thank you, everybody! Thank You, Arielle! I am so grateful. I can swim a lot better now with all that net off me, so I think I will give it a go. I will head for The Coldest Place and try to find some food along the way. My mom should be heading there soon, too. Goodbye, my friends!"

Lily exited the harbor, turned right, and headed up the coast toward Alaska. Everyone hoped for the best.

When the team returned to shore, the news media surrounded them. People from ABC, CBS, NBC, CNN, the *Dana Point Times*, *Orange County Register*, *LA Times*, and more were all there. Eric showed them some of the netting they took off Lily while Dean was walking up the ramp.

Arielle and her mom were waiting for Capt. Dave and gave him a really big hug. The reporters asked the rescuers a lot of questions.

That was when Capt. Dave told all of the reporters, "A thousand dolphins and whales are dying in nets and fishing gear, around the world, every day. EVERY DAY!" he repeated loudly.

The next morning the story of Lily's disentanglement was on the front page of the newspaper. Everyone hoped it was really a happy ending to a sad story. But right after reading the paper, Capt. Dave received a disturbing phone call from his good friend Mike Bursk, the captain of the Sea Explorer at the Ocean Institute.

"She's back," he said.

Lily had returned and was waiting just outside the harbor.

"Come on, Arielle," Capt. Dave said to his daughter. "Let's go see what's going on with Lily."

There was already a dolphin and whale safari scheduled, so all the passengers would get to see Lily, too.

FAST FACTS

More whales, porpoises, and dolphins die every year by getting entangled in fishing gear than from any other cause. Researchers at Duke University and the University of St. Andrews in Scotland have estimated a global annual average of nearly 308,000 deaths per year — or nearly 1,000 per day.

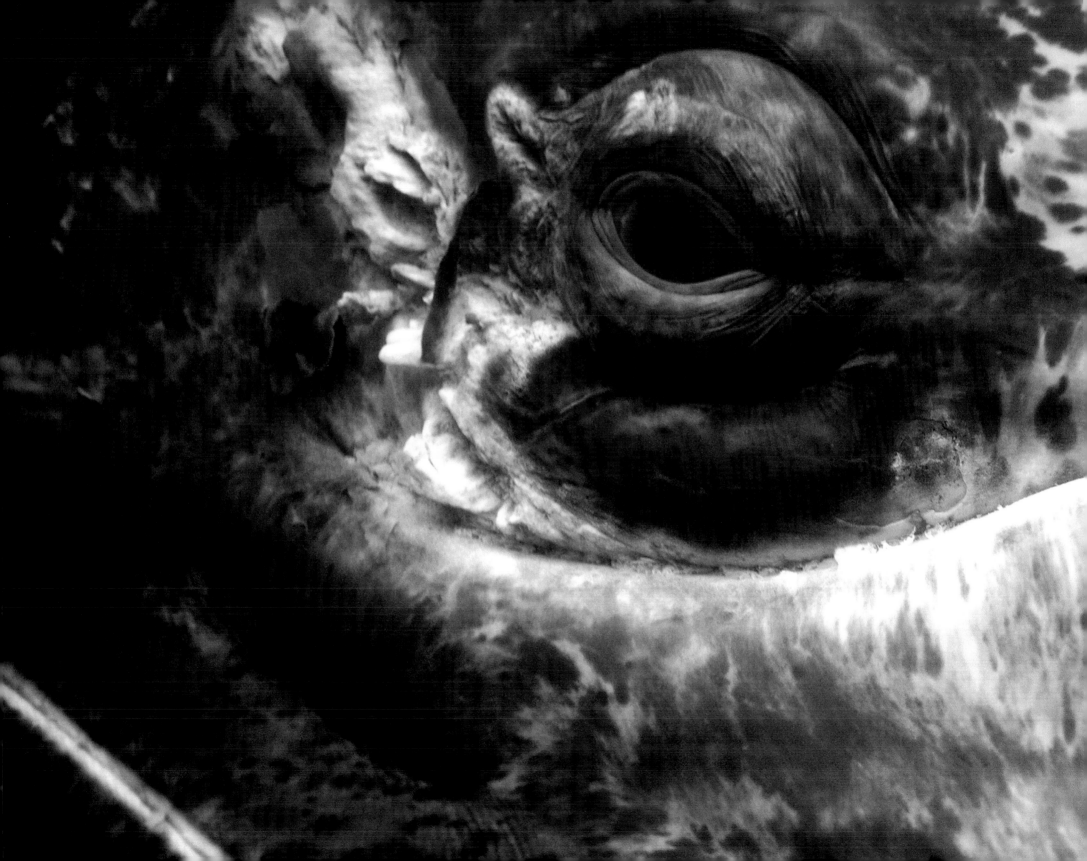

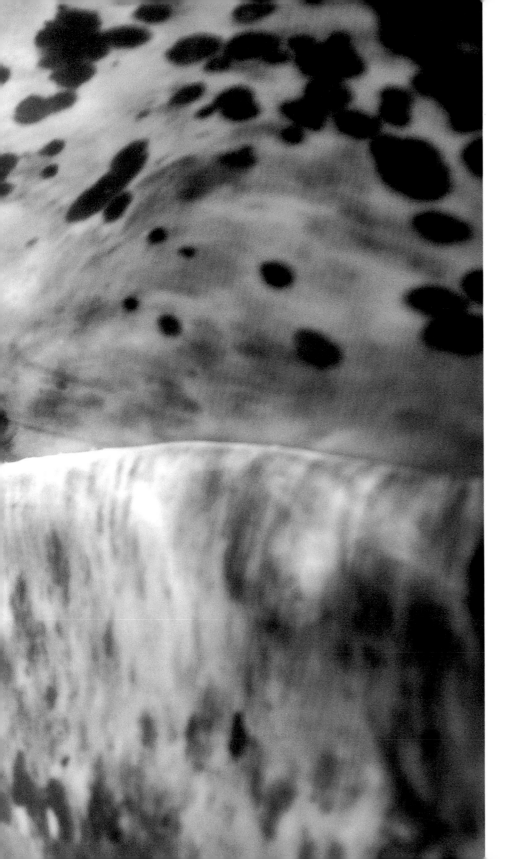

CHAPTER NINE

Can Someone Please Help Lily?

In just a few minutes, the *Manute'a* was outside the harbor jetty. Lily swam right over to the underwater viewing pod to see them. She spoke to Arielle in a quiet voice, "Arielle, I'm afraid I am not going to make it. I'm not going to ever leave here again. I'm just not strong enough."

"No!" Arielle pleaded.

"Yes, little Caretaker. I've gone too long without food. Please don't worry about me. It is my time to go to the Creator. I will be fine, really. I returned today to this harbor for all my relatives and friends, to tell you . . . " Lily's voice choked with emotion, "so many of them have gotten caught in these nets already and some of them, like me, did not make it. You Caretakers are supposed to take care of us—of everything the Creator has given you. Back in the days when there was no killing, no dying and everything was good, he placed us under your authority to rule over us and to take care of us. The Creator gave you hands and a choice. He put you in charge! Can you please, please, tell all the Caretakers of the earth to stop hurting us?"

"I will, Lily. I promise!" Arielle reassured. "My Dad and I will do everything we can to help your friends. But first we are going to help you."

"You can't help me, Arielle. I'm starving, and there is nothing in these waters for me to eat, at least nothing I am strong enough to catch. I can't go another inch. I am too weak."

"No! No! Don't give up! My dad will help you, and I'll talk to Old Dolphin. He's a wise old dolphin. He's the one who saved you and your mom from the killer whales with that danger sound. He'll know what to do! Don't give up, Lily!" Arielle coaxed. "We'll go get some help and be back as soon as we do. I promise!"

"I know you will, Arielle. I know you will try, at least. I trust you, Arielle. You're a good Caretaker."

Lily was very quiet for a long time, and then as Arielle turned to leave, Lily spoke, "I have a joke for you, Arielle. Why was the whale so sad?"

"I don't know, Lily. Why?"

"Because he was a blue whale," Lily said without laughing.

Arielle blinked back tears and climbed out of the underwater viewing pod to tell her dad what Lily had said. Her dad called Mr. Joe, and Mr. Joe said there was nothing more they could do. Unfortunately, there was no way to feed her. The disentanglement was over, so they had to stay at least 100 yards away from Lily from now on. Capt. Dave was not very happy about this, but he told Mr. Joe that he understood and would respect his wishes.

"Dad, we can't just give up. We have to find Old Dolphin—we just have to!" Arielle pleaded.

Capt. Dave nodded. "Okay, little one. Let's go find him."

So they headed out in search of Old Dolphin.

Only a mile and a half away from the harbor they found a huge pod of common dolphins. Old Dolphin was a bottlenose, so Arielle knew he wouldn't be in this pod. Maybe one of them knew where he might be.

Arielle could hear the dolphins closest to her repeating to themselves over and over, "I will not go over to the boat. I will not boat surf. I will not go over to the boat. Must find food. No bow riding. The needs of the pod come first. I-will-not-go-over-to-the-boat! I am strong! I have self-control! I have free will! I- am- my- own- dolphin!"

But in the end, the dolphins could not resist the boat. Soon they were all racing for the front of the boat crying, "Eee–haaaa!"

There were over 5,000 common dolphins in this herd. With so many dolphins, Arielle began to wonder if maybe these dolphins might be able to do something to help Lily.

First Mate Mark dropped the hydrophone in the water, and they towed the array behind the boat, so everyone could hear the whistles and clicks of the dolphins through speakers all over the boat. But only Arielle understood what they were saying. She heard all of the dolphins singing a song as they swam along:

Yeah, we're dolphins, And we love to play.

'Cause we're dolphins, And we play all day.

'Cause we're dolphins, And we work together,

And we live together And we stick together.

'Cause we're dolphins. Yeah, we're dolphins.

So Arielle went down into the X-Pod, the underwater viewing pod set up for experimental interspecies communication. She hoped to talk to a few of them—to tell them what was going on and to ask them to help.

The microphone sent out a sound through special speakers located inside of the pod, this sound could also barely be heard by the dolphins and whales that were already right next to the boat, but Arielle figured it would be easier than yelling to them.

Who showed near the underwater viewing pod? None other than Casper the albino dolphin.

Arielle was so happy she squealed! Casper was a friendly dolphin. He would definitely help, she thought.

Casper looked inside. "I suppose you're here about Lily?" he asked.

"Yes. How did you know?" wondered Arielle.

"I heard it through the sardine-vine," the white dolphin stated.

"Can you help her?"

"Well, maybe. She's hungry, right? How about if we scare up some sardines for her?"

"Well, I don't know. Maybe, if they were easy for her to catch. You know, she doesn't normally have to chase her food much. She usually eats amphipods. But I guess if you made it easy enough for her to catch some sardines . . . but don't forget, she can't swim very fast because she's hurt," Arielle urged.

"Say no more. We will get it done," assured Casper.

Before Casper could tell the rest of the pod, another dolphin grumbled, "Ah, excuse me, but who died and made you king, O Great Albino One? Any sardines I see, I am going to eat, not save 'em for some baleen hole-head that wouldn't give *us* the time of day if *she* didn't need *our* help!"

"That's right!" accused another.

"Oh, please help her," Arielle pleaded. She will die for sure if she doesn't get something to eat very soon."

"Well, why don't you feed her then?" challenged another common dolphin.

"We would," said Arielle, "but we don't have any amphipods around here, and she only eats live food. If you could chase some live sardines over near her and keep them from running away, then maybe she could catch some. Could you please help?" Arielle pleaded.

"So, let me get this straight," another common dolphin protested. "You want all of us to work together as a team to herd the fish, which we always do anyway, but then you want us to not eat them, but instead drive them all the way back to the harbor for a whale? Not for the good of the pod, but for the good of a whale? Talk to the flipper, I say. Let the whales take care of themselves. We have enough trouble taking care of our own!"

"Hey, excuse me," rebuked Casper, "but dolphins are whales, O Selfish One! Don't listen to him, Arielle. He's not our leader! We don't have a leader! I say we should help Lily!"

"Yeah, me too!" agreed a bow-riding dolphin.

"Me three," urged another.

"Me four," concurred a fourth.

"Me . . . "

"Hey, everybody, look!" whistled a dolphin. "Sardines!"

"Okay, folks, it's dinner time!" someone shouted. "But let's save some for Lily, too. We'll start working 'em toward the harbor!"

"Okay!" agreed one dolphin.

"Yes!" said another.

"Amen!" proclaimed another.

"That's right," responded a different one.

And just like that, they decided as a group to help. Some wouldn't, at first, but as the majority moved forward, even the most opposed began to join in as well. And they sang:

Yeah, we're dolphins, And we work together.
Cause we're dolphins, And we eat together.
'Cause we're dolphins. Yeah, we're dolphins.

Then they stopped singing and all that Arielle could hear through the towed hydrophone array were the clicks of the dolphins' sonar, echolocating off the sardines. They did work together, going under the fish and chasing them up toward the surface where they could better control them, where there was no escape for the sardines. The whole dolphin herd began driving the school of fish toward Dana Point Harbor, eating some as they went.

Each dolphin would zero in on just one sardine in the middle of thousands and follow that specific sardine until he caught it in his mouth and swallowed it. The sardines would leap out of the water trying to escape the dolphins.

Arielle heard the sardines, one after another, affirming their creed, "Remember, stay together and live another day!" said one.

"Okay, Slimy Ones, stay calm! Blend in, and stay alive!" said another.

"Safety in numbers!" cried a third.

"Don't panic and run. It will only get you noticed!" affirmed a fourth.

One of the sardines spotted Arielle in the underwater viewing pod and declared, "Hey, look guys! People in a can!"

Then, without warning, a blue shark appeared and cut right into the middle of the sardines.

"*It's a shark!*" screamed several sardines.

"Forget what I said, scaly ones!" said a frightened sardine.

"Swim for it!" said another. "Every sardine for himself!"

"Hold together, you chickens of the sea," said a third.

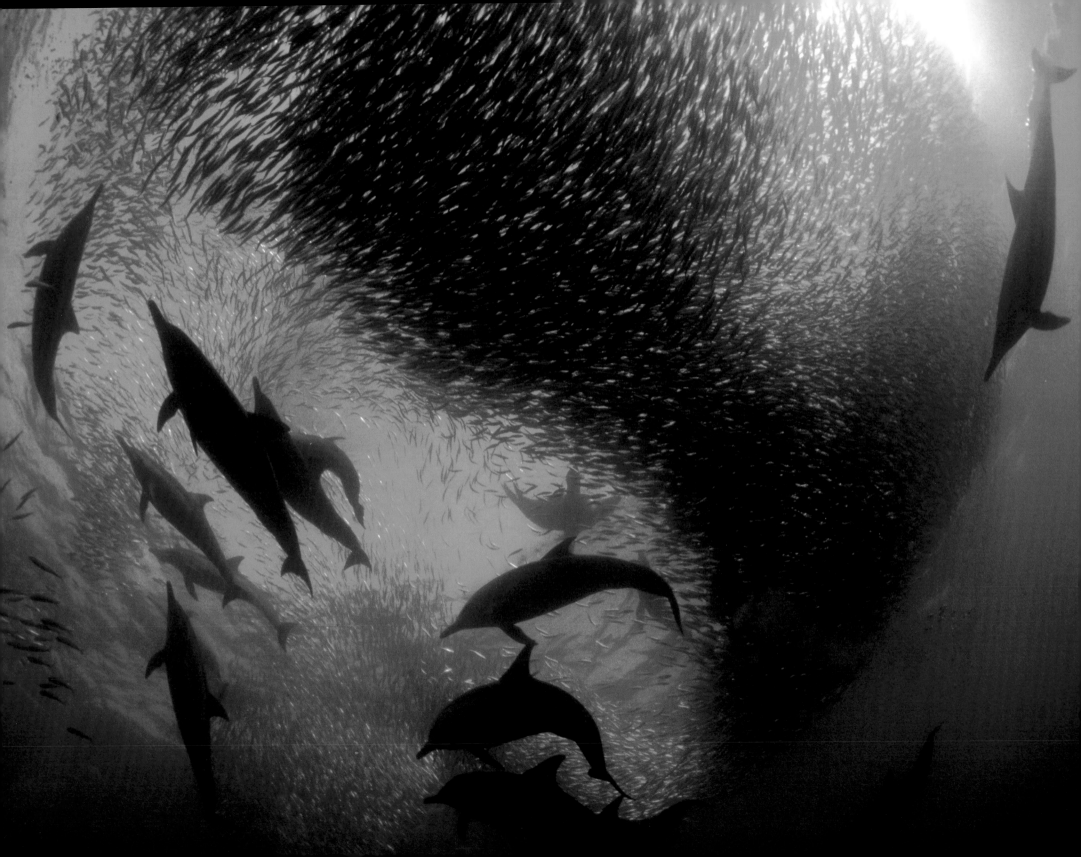

"I'd like to make an announcement," said Smiley the shark, to all the common dolphins. "These sardines are mine. My buddies are coming, and we'll take it from here, but you dolphins are welcome to stick around. We'd love to have you stay for dinner."

"Shark!!!" the dolphins said to each other as they abandoned the sardines and charged away singing:

Yeah, we're dolphins, And we're scared together.
'Cause we're dolphins, And we love to run away.
'Cause we're dolphins, And we're scared of sharks all day.
'Cause we're dolphins. Yeah, we're dolphins.

All the dolphins leapt into the air and porpoised full speed away from the sharks and away from the *Manute'a* and away from the sardines. It was a dolphin stampede!

At the back of the pod Arielle spotted her old friend Cooper. Cooper was a fast swimmer, but he was not quite able to swim as fast as the others when they were porpoising. Cooper had been born with a deformity, but Cooper never gave up.

Arielle called out to Cooper as he was passing by *Manute'a*, "Why are all you dolphins afraid of this one shark?"

"It's not sharks we're scared of exactly. It's Smiley!"

"What!" cried Arielle, "I've seen dolphins and sharks feeding on the same sardines before without killing each other! Besides, if you dolphins worked together, you could easily defeat the shark. I guess you never watched *Flipper* or the Discovery Channel?"

"Sorry, but you don't know Smiley, He's a mean, unpredictable shark!" said Cooper.

"Come back and help Lily!"

"Sorry Arielle, I've got to go! I can't get separated from the pod, or I could die."

Arielle helplessly watched as Lily's nourishment disappeared, as the sardines, pursued by Smiley, vanished in the now murky blue-green water.

Then Capt. Dave spotted a blow that shot thirty feet into the air. It was a blue whale, the largest animal that has ever lived, just up ahead.

It was a big whale, even for a blue whale. It was over three times the size of Lily and made the fifty-foot *Manute'a* look small. Arielle recognized this particular blue whale when it came straight over to their boat. It was Big Al.

She told Al about Lily's problem and asked if he might know what they could do to help her.

In a deep voice that rattled the underwater windows and shook the whole boat he said, "I know a place about a fifth of a day's swim straight off your harbor. There are amphipods there, lots of them. I have seen gray whales, like your friend, feasting there."

"How will we get her there?" asked Arielle. "My dad can't tow her there. They will arrest him if he tries. He can't do anything. He's not even allowed to get closer than 100 yards."

Al's voice thundered, "Silence, while I think."

But Arielle kept talking. "I'm trying to find Old Dolphin. I think he might know what to do, but I haven't been able to find him."

With that, Al raised his giant tail flukes out of the water and dove straight down under the water as the passengers and a nearby paddleboarder watched, and he disappeared. The only thing left was his footprint, a giant smooth spot on the water created by his powerful tail flukes moving up and down.

"Hey, don't go away," Arielle cried. "I need you to help me, to help Lily! Don't you care? Come back, Big Al! Lily needs you!"

Al exploded out of the water near the boat. He turned and headed straight at the boat, much to the surprise and delight of the passengers.

FAST FACTS

According to Cascadia Research and NOAA, California has the largest concentration of blue whales on earth.

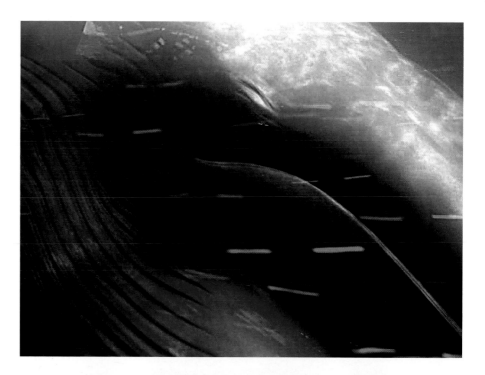

Big Al swam straight over to the underwater viewing pod and looked Arielle in the eye.

"How *dare* you question *my* motives! You should know better, young Caretaker!" Al roared angrily, rattling the boat. "In the days before the knowledge was given, Lily would have meant nothing to me. But now? Knowledge brings choices! We will all be held accountable for our choices one day! I don't know how to help your friend, but I know someone who can!"

The entire ocean trembled as he called out in a deep voice that could be heard a thousand miles away, "*Old Dolphin!*"

With that Al surfaced, took a last breath, and began a deep dive. Water poured off his tail flukes like a waterfall as he disappeared.

FAST FACTS

Blue whales make a low frequency sound that, under the right circumstances, can travel over a thousand miles underwater.

Arielle and her dad kept looking for Old Dolphin, but they couldn't find him, or his constant companion, Yard Sale Dolphin, anywhere. Arielle was out on the front of the boat when she overheard her dad talking to Barry on the radio.

"Dave, Lily is on the beach at Doheny," said Barry, in a tinny voice over the radio.

"She's dead," Barry said.

Capt. Dave was stunned and did not respond.

"Did you read me?" asked Barry as he watched Lily get rolled over by a wave.

"Roger," said Capt. Dave sadly.

"She made it to the soft sand at Doheny beach," Barry said, choking back his emotion. "She's gone. I heard her make some kind of a sound. I swear she was trying to talk to me, to thank us for trying to help her."

Arielle tried not to believe Barry's words.

He must be wrong, she thought.

When they reached the harbor entrance near Doheny beach, they could see for themselves what was happening. They watched as a man attached a rope near Lily's tail flukes.

They slowly pulled her lifeless body off the beach as hundreds of people said goodbye to Lily from shore.

Arielle was devastated. Never again would she be able to talk with her friend Lily. As the reality sank in, she lay down on the "Eye Spy Dolphin Net" and began to cry.

Just then Old Dolphin swam up under the front of the boat as the passengers and Capt. Dave looked on from above.

"What's wrong, Arielle?" Old Dolphin asked in a concerned voice.

"Lily is dead," said Arielle, in between uncontrollable sobbing.

Old Dolphin smiled, "Who says she's dead."

"I saw her on the beach."

"So did lots of other Caretakers, but don't you believe it, Arielle. Lily is alive!"

"No! You're just trying to make me feel better."

Don't give up on Lily, Arielle. She is not dead yet. He paused to let his words sink in. "She's only pretending!"

Arielle stopped crying and looked at Old Dolphin through tear-filled eyes.

"You see," explained Old Dolphin, "Yard Sale Dolphin and I overheard Lily telling her whole sad story to you. Then we ran into Big Al. We needed to find a way to get Lily out to Al's amphipods, but how? We thought and thought, and then it hit me like a tail slap.

Whenever a whale dies and goes to the Creator, you Caretakers always tow the body ten of your miles out to sea—and that is right where Al's amphipods are! That was the answer! Lily can hold her breath for over ten minutes, so after about six hidden breaths, off they went! They towed her out to sea, Arielle! Lily did it perfectly—she even turned on her side, so she was facing away from the crowd, so no one would see her blow holes open and close. She's on her way to a feast, I tell you! But she is awfully weak. Yard Sale Dolphin went with her to help since I'm too slow to keep up with the boat. I sure hope she makes it."

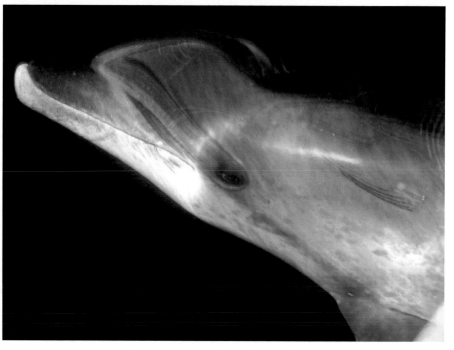

Arielle was so happy she felt as if she could fly! But then her thoughts turned to worries: "Will Lily really be okay? She's so weak she can barely swim! How will she survive being towed out to sea? What if they notice she's alive? They might untie her and let her go; then, she would never make it to the feeding grounds." She pushed her fears aside because for now, Arielle had something bigger to grab hold of—hope!

Meanwhile, Yard Sale Dolphin was quietly swimming along next to Lily as she was being towed out to sea. Yard Sale knew exactly how to handle himself in emergency situations like this, being a former Navy dolphin. He had served in the Persian Gulf as part of the Navy Marine Mammal Program that has located mines and hostile divers underwater, in every war since Vietnam.

Normally a dolphin of few words, Yard Sale Dolphin decided to tell Lily a joke he had learned in the military to help her relax and not be so frightened.

"I know a great whale joke," he declared.

"A joke, oh good," Lily said weakly. "What is it?" she asked as the boat continued dragging her backward through the water. Lily was thankful to have something, anything to think about, instead of her present situation.

Because of all the engine noise, no one on the boat could hear their interspecies communication.

"Okay," began Yard Sale Dolphin, "so a little female Caretaker was learning about whales from a so-called expert. The expert told her it was physically impossible for a whale to swallow a human being because its throat was too small. The little Caretaker girl thought about this and said, 'I thought Jonah was swallowed by a whale.'

"Irritated, the expert repeated that a whale could not swallow a human. It was physically impossible.

"The little girl said, 'When I get to heaven, I will ask Jonah.'

"So the expert jokingly asked, 'Well, what if Jonah went to hell?'

"The little girl thought for a moment, then respectfully replied, 'Well, then maybe you could ask him.'"

Yard Sale Dolphin and Lily both laughed.

"Okay, I've got one," Lily said. "What is a shark's favorite kind of sandwich?"

"I don't know," said Yard Sale Dolphin

"Peanut butter and jellyfish," said Lily.

CHAPTER TEN

Lily Says Goodbye

A few weeks later, Arielle and her mom and dad were out on a dolphin and whale safari when they spotted Old Dolphin and Yard Sale Dolphin.

Old Dolphin shouted to the boat, "Arielle! Have you seen Lily?" as he breached over and over near the *Manute'a* and near Capt. Dave's other catamaran sailboat, *Dolphinsafari*.

"No!" said Arielle, "Have you seen her?"

"No! Old Dolphin replied, "Lily was feeding and feeding and feeding on amphipods, but she disappeared, and now I can't find her! I hope she's okay! I heard through the sardine-vine that she was well enough to head back to The Coldest Place and that she's coming to see you to say goodbye. Maybe we got here ahead of her."

Arielle was thrilled to hear this, but she had a problem. The boat was almost back to the harbor, and she was supposed to help package meals for hungry children in Africa and Haiti with her mom and others from her church.

"Mom, Lily is coming to see me!" said Arielle to her mother. "Can I go back out with Dad on his next trip to see her?"

Her mom thought about it for several seconds and said, "Yes, you can, Arielle. It's up to you, but I thought you wanted to help the kids in Africa and Haiti? We're supposed to be packaging meals in half an hour. You can't do both."

"I know, Mom, but I really, really want to see Lily again," Arielle reasoned.

Her mom watched her quietly, "The decision is yours to make, Arielle."

When they reached the dock, all the passengers disembarked and her mom hugged her goodbye and started to walk down the dock. Arielle looked at her dad and back at her mom. She wanted so much to see Lily, but she knew there were poor children who needed help in Haiti and Africa. She remembered what Old Dolphin and Big Al had said about making good choices. She knew what a good Caretaker would do, and she knew that was what God would want her to do. So she said goodbye to her dad and ran down the dock to her mom. These children needed her more than Lily did.

They spent two hours packaging meals and it was all done through an organization called Kids Around The World. They all had lots of fun. Arielle and her mom then rushed home to see if her dad had caught up with Lily.

They got on her mom's computer, so they could watch the live broadcast from the boat just in time to see...

FAST FACTS
Half of the profits from this book will go to charities like Kids Around The World.

. . . Yard Sale Dolphin and Old Dolphin jumping in the sunset. Old Dolphin swam over to the boat.

He went right up next to the underwater viewing pod.

"Arielle, I hope you are watching!" The old bottlenose dolphin said to the video camera in the underwater viewing pod. "You will never believe who is here!" Arielle held her breath and kept her eyes glued on the computer monitor in hopes of spotting Lily on one of the boat's cameras.

A whale surfaced near the boat—a small gray whale.

The whale was completely focused on its journey. It swam in a straight line, never veering to the left or to the right. This whale could not waste any of its precious energy doing anything but heading for The Coldest Place, where there was plenty of food to eat.

Then the whale turned around and swam toward the *Manute'a*.

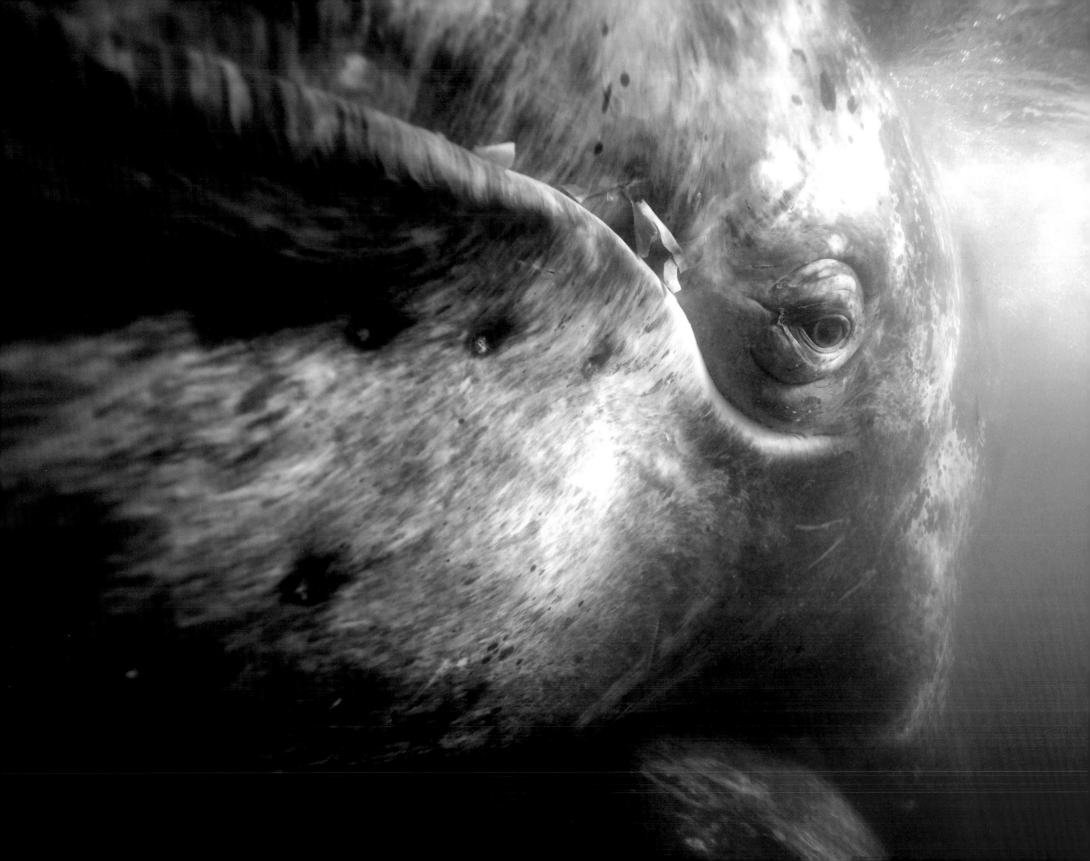

This young giant came over to the boat and stuck its massive head into view of the camera, and with Arielle watching from home, asked a riddle: "How do you keep a Caretaker in suspense from the warm season until the cold season?"

Arielle was giddy with excitement at hearing Lily's voice again.

Lily paused for a moment and then answered her own question, "I'll tell you next winter, Arielle, the Caretaker that I love!" Then Lily laughed loud and long like her beloved Uncle Mike.

Arielle thought about it for a moment, then she burst out laughing, too. "Yes!" she cried, "I will see Lily again, next winter."

Old Dolphin and Yard Sale Dolphin swam over to Lily as she left the camera's view, "Do you think she was watching?" Lily asked the dolphin duo.

"I am absolutely certain that she heard every word," Old Dolphin replied. Yard Sale Dolphin nodded in agreement.

Lily arched her back and dove down under the water and disappeared, followed by Old Dolphin and Yard Sale Dolphin, who arched their backs for a deep dive and vanished as well.

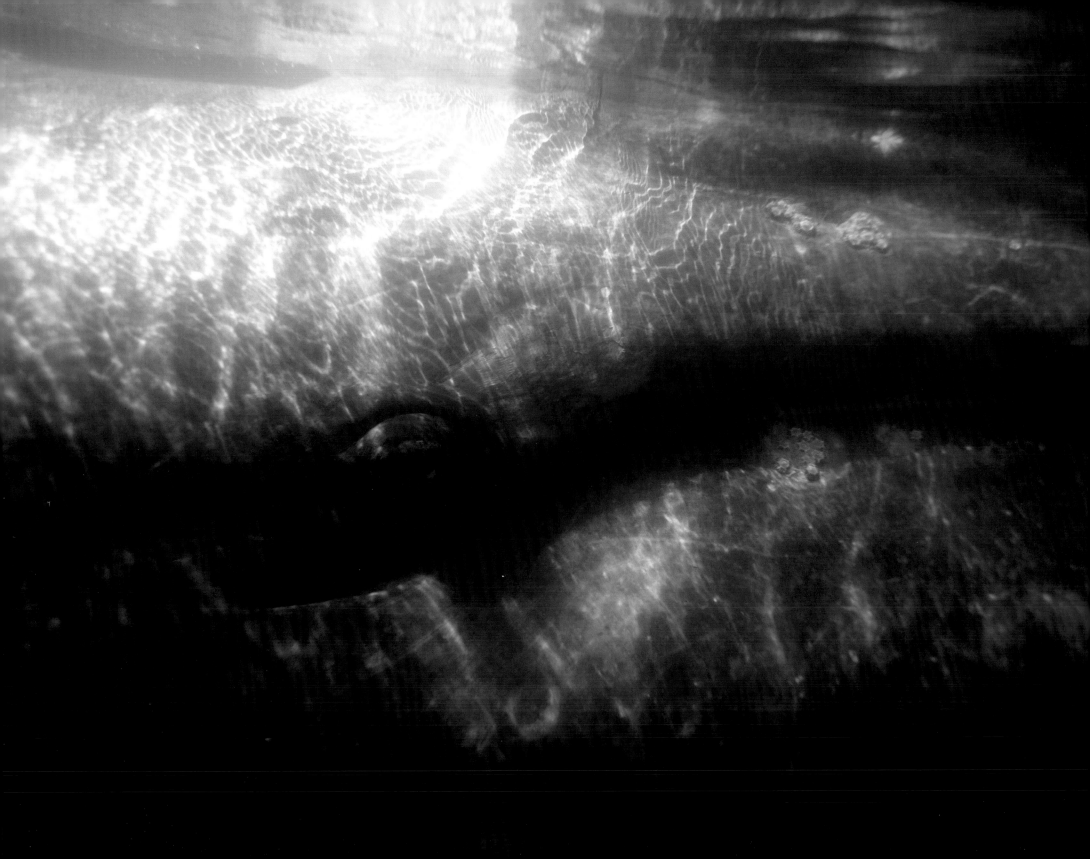

Then another, much bigger, whale came into camera view. This leviathan began to speak in what seemed like a stern, almost angry tone as Arielle and her mom stared at the computer monitor in disbelief, though only Arielle could actually decipher the meaning of all the whale's grunts and groans.

"Arielle, I've heard about you, young Caretaker! You are the reason my daughter was able to break her promise never to trust the Caretakers outside of The Lagoon! I had made this rule because you Caretakers have shown us that you are not to be trusted; with your traps and harpoons and trash everywhere! But I've learned that some of you are different."

"*Thank you!* You are a good Caretaker, Arielle. We will never forget you! We will tell the story of you and the other good Caretakers to our brothers and sisters, from The Coldest Place to The Warmest Place! I tell you the truth: What you have done for my Lily will never be forgotten!" proclaimed Lily's mom.

She surfaced next to the boat and exhaled loudly through her two closeable blowholes, getting the passengers wet with the mist. Satisfied, she dove straight down and disappeared. After she left, the only shape that could be seen on the water was a silhouette of Catalina Island in the distance.

The sun said goodbye, too, as *Manute'a* turned and headed for home. The people on board, who had been standing with excitement, now, finally, sat back down, went inside the cabin and relaxed. Some looked at their cameras for the images they had just captured, and some just sat silently, satisfied with their most amazing encounter with whales and dolphins. As the high-speed catamaran sailboat sped back toward Dana Point Harbor a gray whale fluked in their wake, unseen by anyone.

"You were wrong," said Arielle to her mom playfully, "I got to do both."

Her mom looked at her and smiled. "Yes, you did!" she said, giving her daughter a hug. I am proud of you. You made a good, but difficult, choice."

Arielle felt good inside.

Then Arielle, and her mom at home, and her dad on *Manute'a*, watched the sun vanish in a silent explosion of color. They were thankful for all that God had made, and for all that He had allowed them to see.

What can we do to help Lily's friends?

Step 1. The problem is that an estimated 308,000 dolphins and whales die because of fishing gear entanglement every year worldwide. This is nearly 1,000 a day. Many people, myself included, thought that this problem was solved years ago when the dolphin-safe labels were put on cans of tuna. At that time, back in 1990, the U.S. tuna companies agreed to utilize only safe fishing practices. Unfortunately there are still non-dolphin-safe tuna nets, as well as many other types of nets and fishing gear, still entangling dolphins and whales. While there are many good people trying to solve this problem with improved fishing practices in the U. S. and other countries, there is still a problem. Like many problems, awareness is the first step to solving it. We must help those already working on solutions by first becoming aware of the problem and helping others become aware. Then we can join in the solution. I realize now from talking to many of our Captain Dave's Dolphin and Whale Safari passengers that they are, for the most part, like I was, unaware of the severity of this problem. Since our passengers are interested enough in whales and dolphins to come out to see them, and yet most know little of this epidemic, I feel certain that very few people in the general public are aware of how bad this issue really is.

You can do something about it. You can help raise awareness by sharing this book with others and by going to our website www.TheCaretakers.org to learn more about helping Lily's friends. At our website you can watch a short video about the real-life Lily, and if you "like" this video on Facebook and other social media sites, many people will learn about this entanglement issue. Then, together, we can help make change happen before it is too late.

Step 2. I believe that rescuing whales caught in nets is not enough! We have to go to the source. Having some countries restricting their nets and where and how they fish while others fish unrestricted is not enough! Yes, reducing by-catch (by-catch refers to the unintended animals caught or killed in the nets, such as seabirds, sea turtles, sea lions, seals, other fish, and, of course, dolphins and whales) in any one place will help animals in those areas, but many whales, like Lily, cross borders into high by-catch areas. Fishing practices in some of those countries might only be improved by economic pressure. So to that end we must work toward getting all our fish labeled so we can tell how it was caught and how much by-catch was associated with catching any particular fish. For example, we could have a scale from 0-5, 0 meaning zero by-catch and 5 meaning extremely high by-catch. Armed with knowledge of the problem and choices, I believe the public will make good choices, like they did in 1990, and force the markets to buy and sell fish caught with the least by-catch. Learn more and

sign the petition to get fish labeled at www.TheCaretakers.org.

Step 3. Ask how the fish were caught when you are in a market or in a restaurant. If enough people ask, merchants will start asking, too, and they will make good choices with respect to what they buy. Also, buy dolphin-safe tuna caught by U.S. companies, all of which have promised to use safe fishing practices for tuna. And for now, if you live in the U.S., buy U. S.-caught fish whenever possible, as we have some of the strictest laws and best fishing practices to prevent by-catch. But unfortunately we still have by-catch problems to solve, even in the U.S. **We have a plan. Join us at www.TheCaretakers.org. Educate, then legislate. Boycott the by-catch. Thanks.**

—Capt. Dave

Grownup Stuff

What Really Happened to Lily the Whale?

Was she really caught in a net? Yes. Her disentanglement shown in this book really happened pretty much as it is explained in the book. You can go to Capt. Dave's website Dolphinsafari.com and watch news footage showing the disentanglement. All photos of it in this book are authentic. Many of the photos of the disentanglement were donated by the *Orange County Register* and the *Dana Point Times*, and some were taken by Capt. Dave and others.

THE ORANGE COUNTY

REGISTER

PRICE: 75 CENTS   THURSDAY, MAY 13, 2010   FOUNDED IN 1905

BUSINESS
Step right up
Buy shaved ice, cupcakes and more from food trucks

LIFE * FOOD
Wield spears

PHOTOS: MICHAEL GOULDING, THE ORANGE COUNTY REGISTER
Dave Anderson, left, and Eric Otjen watch Dean Gomersall go over the side Wednesday while clearing netting on the body of a gray whale in Dana Point Harbor.

TEAM FREES LILLY
Rescuers hope a whale, cleared of nets, swims to Alaska.

As hundreds watched in Dana Point Harbor, a team from SeaWorld San Diego and the Pacific Marine Mammal Center in Laguna Beach worked for more than two hours Wednesday to cut gill netting and nylon rope off a young gray whale's body that was believed to have im-

Did she really come into Dana Point Harbor looking for help? Lily really did end up, the morning of the rescue, right in front of the very building where Capt. Dave, Dean, Capt. Tom, Mark, Barry, and others were trained by NOAA. Many people believe she came into the harbor looking for someone to help her. What we do know is that when whales are weak and are having trouble keeping afloat, they often beach themselves as a last resort. There was a nice beach for Lily to rest on just outside the harbor (which is where she ended up later), but Lily did not have to keep coming in and out of the harbor like she did. It is impossible to know for certain why she did so.

Did she actually die, like the papers and news stories reported? There is the real life Lily and the fictional Lily. The fictional Lily is most definitely alive. As far as the other Lily, she expired on the beach at Doheny two days after the disentanglement and was towed ten miles out to sea an hour later. All photos of this event are real. However if you are like Arielle in the story and believe that Lily and the other animals are able to talk to people, then you will also know that she did actually fake her death.

Was she really born in a lagoon in Baja California, Mexico? We don't know for sure, but most likely she was. Most gray whales are born in these lagoons, or on the way down to them.

Did she really have an encounter with killer whales and hunters in Russia? We don't really know if this happened to Lily, but it is very possible she encountered them. It is estimated that as many as thirty-five percent of gray whale calves are killed by killer whales and this does not include the ones who were attacked but got away. You may think it unlikely for a gray whale to have had so much misfortune in such a short life, but please read the following newspaper story from the *Times Standard* in Eureka, California, written a little over two months before Lily ended up in Dana Point. This whale was the same size and age as Lily. It is possible that Lily may have even met her during her migration. Lily's story in this book is a combination of this whale's true life history and what we know about Lily's true life history.

Gray whale washed up on Humboldt County beach may have been harpooned off Russia

John Driscoll/The Times-Standard 03/03/2010

The gray whale washed up on Dry Lagoon beach on Feb. 2 was hardly an unusual sight. But when the mammal rolled over in the surf 11 days later, the shaft of a harpoon could be seen jutting from its flesh.

Humboldt State University Marine Mammal Stranding Network members removed the harpoon and found the tip of another harpoon embedded in the whale. They also collected additional tissue samples to turn in to the National Marine Fisheries Service for investigation, which has recently produced some results.

Commercial whaling has been outlawed by the United States since the 1970s. There is a limited harvest of bowhead whales by native Alaskans. (Edit) The harpoon appears to be of the type used by Alaskan and Russian natives for subsistence hunting, officials say.

"This whale had probably traveled 3,500 miles from where it was likely targeted to where it ended up," said marine biologist Dawn Goley at Humboldt State University.

Goley said biologists were unable to determine the cause of death of the 27-foot female whale, and initially suspected that it had succumbed to natural causes before the harpoon was exposed. The whale was likely a yearling on its first migration from feeding grounds in the Bering Sea or Chukchi Sea between Alaska and Russia, to Baja California, Goley said.

Alaskan natives can only target bowhead whales for subsistence use under regulations set by the International Whaling Commission, and killed about 35 to 75 whales a year between 2000 and 2008. The native people of the far northeast Russian territory of Chukotka—mainly Yupik, Eskimo and Chukchi people—are allowed to kill up to 140 gray whales each year between 2008 to 2012.

National Marine Fisheries Service Special Agent Tim Broadman said that the harpoon found in the Dry Lagoon whale was not a commercial whaling tool, and appears to match those used by the natives in the Chukotka region of Russia. He said that native whalers must record when whales are struck and then get away, and the whaling commission does have a record of a lost whale from that region.

Broadman said that the whale appears to have gone through quite an ordeal—even aside from being harpooned.

The young whale had teeth marks consistent with an orca attack, and also a kinked spine.

"It's heart-wrenching in a way," he said.

The host country pleads the case for native subsistence hunting before the whaling commission, which sets quotas for a five-year period. The commission then determines how many whales can be taken without harming the populations of the whales in question.

"It's based on science," said National Oceanic and Atmospheric Administration spokesman Scott Smullen. "How much can that stock take from subsistence hunting?"

Gray whales were nearly driven to extinction by commercial whaling in the 1850s and again in the early 1900s, according to the American Cetacean Society. The eastern North Pacific gray whale was protected by the whaling commission in 1947, and their population has recovered to between 19,000 and 23,000 individuals, which is probably close to their original population size, according to the society.

In the rationale provided by Russia for the 2008-2012 time frame, it says that harvesting and eating whales is essential to the survival and cultural unity of the Chukotka people. There is no substitute for whale meat, the paper reads, which represents some 90 percent of the meat in native diets. The native hunts claim about 126 whales a year, and are limited by lack of boats, equipment, and trained crews.

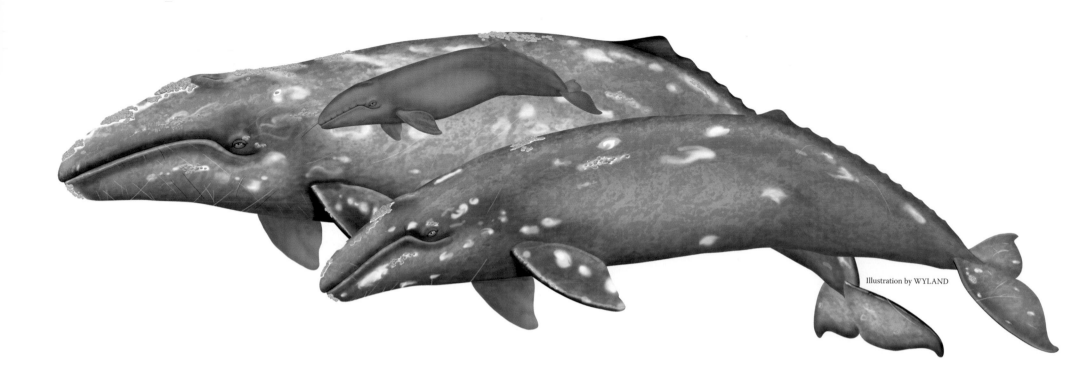

Illustration by WYLAND

Lily, her mom, and Uncle Mike are California gray whales: *Eschrictius robustus.*

Kingdom: *Animalia*

Phylum: *Chordata*

Class: *Mammalia*

Order: *Cetacea*

Suborder: *Mysticeti*

Family: *Eschrichtiidae*

Genus: *Eschrichtius*

Species: *robustus*

Species Description: The gray whale (*Eschrichtius robustus*) was first known to science on the basis of a subfossil skeleton from Sweden described by Lilljeborg in 1861. The family and genus names refer to the Danish zoology professor Daniel Eschricht, and the species name means "strong" or "oaken" in Latin. Gray whales are mysticetes, or baleen whales. Gray whales are the only species in the family *Eschrichtiidae*.

Description: The flukes (tails) are broad, often spanning more than 9 feet (3 m) wide. Gray Whales have the fewest baleen plates of any whale species, with 130-180 yellowish white plates on each side of the mouth.

Size: 36-50 feet (11-15 m). Males are slightly smaller than females; maximum body weight is about 99,000 lbs (45,000 kg).

Behavior: Migrating gray whales move steadily in one direction, breathing and diving in predictable patterns. They do not live in pods and commonly travel alone or in small, unstable groups, although large aggregations can occur on both the feeding and breeding grounds. They usually stay underwater about 4 minutes on average, though they can hold their breath much longer. Normal migration speed is about 4 knots, but they can swim much faster if necessary. Gray whales are often very relaxed and curious, even playful, in the lagoons in Baja, and they are usually very focused and occasionally curious and playful during their migration.

Except for mother-calf pairs, associations between individuals are relatively fluid. Breaching and other surface behaviors are common, especially in the lagoons.

Feeding gray whales are usually alone or in small groups, but normally in near proximity to relatively high numbers (10s to 100s).

Gray whales produce sounds including moans, rumbles, and growls. The most prevalent call is a series of knocking sounds.

Migration/Range: Gray whales (eastern North Pacific population) undertake one of the longest annual migrations of any mammal, traveling some 9,300-12,500 miles (15,000-20,000 km) round trip. By late November, most whales are moving south from summer feeding areas (Chukchi, Beaufort, and the northwestern Bering Sea) to winter calving areas (the west coast of Baja California, Mexico, and the southeastern Gulf of California). The northward migration begins about mid-February, and most whales arrive at the summer feeding grounds between May and June. Most of the gray whales pass by Dana Point from January 1–April 15.

Gestation: 12 to 13 months

Birth/calving season: Late December-early February. Females calve at intervals of at least two years. The western population is often every third or fourth year.

Litter size: single calf

Neonate (birth to four weeks) size: 15-16 feet (4.6 - 4.9 m) long, 1500-2000 lbs. (680-920 kg)

Age at Weaning: 7-9 months

Age they are able to reproduce: 6-12 years of age

Lifespan: unknown, estimated 40-80 years. The average and maximum life span of gray whales is unknown, although one female was estimated at 75-80 years old after death (Jones and Swartz, 2002).

Diet: primarily suction-feeders, consuming benthic amphipods on or near the seafloor. They are sometimes known to consume cumaceans, mysids, shrimp, mobile amphipods, crab larvae, and herring eggs. Their main food is benthic amphipods which are in short supply on much of their long journey. These whales eat very little on their migration, relying instead on their stored reserves from feeding nonstop all summer in the Arctic.

Threats: entanglements in fishing gear, environmental degradation—including exposure to contaminants and disturbance by shipping and noise (e.g. seismic surveys)

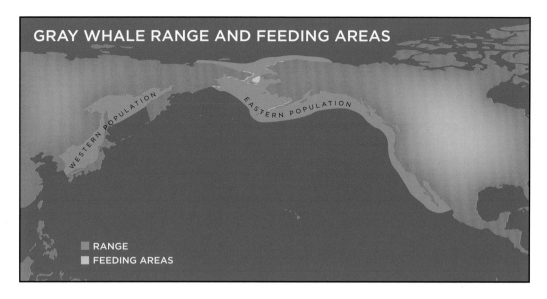

GRAY WHALE RANGE AND FEEDING AREAS

WESTERN POPULATION

EASTERN POPULATION

■ RANGE
■ FEEDING AREAS

related to offshore oil and gas development. The effect of climate change on gray whales and their habitat, especially the notable reduction of sea ice and increasing water temperatures in the Arctic, is yet to be determined. Killer whales (*Orcinus orca*) are the only non-human predator of gray whales. Preliminary estimates have suggested that predation by mammal-eating "transient" killer whales may be responsible for mortalities constituting up to 35% of the average annual calf production of California gray whales (Barrett-Lennard et al. 2005), but there is substantial uncertainty about assumptions underpinning this estimate. Nonetheless, it is clear that if the "transient" killer whale population continues to increase in the eastern Pacific (Ford et al. 2007), the potential for impact on gray whales will also increase.

Distribution: Two normally isolated geographic distributions of gray whales in the North Pacific Ocean—the Eastern North Pacific stock, found along the west coast of North America, and the Western North Pacific or "Korean" stock, found along the coast of eastern Asia—have been observed commingling.

Status: All marine mammals, including gray whales, are protected under the Marine Mammal Protection Act of 1972, as amended. As of 1994, the Eastern North Pacific stock of gray whale is no longer listed as endangered under the Endangered Species Act of 1973.

The Western North Pacific stock of gray whales has not recovered. It is listed as "endangered" under the ESA and "depleted" under the MMPA.

IUCN status (International Union for Conservation of Nature): Western North Pacific population is "critically endangered" with an estimated 130 individuals; Eastern North Pacific population is of "least concern" with about 20,000 individuals estimated.

Gray whales used to be found on the east coast of the U.S. but were extirpated (eliminated, wiped out) by whalers who also nearly wiped out the gray whales on the California coast as well before the gray whales were protected by the U.S. in 1936. North Atlantic populations of gray whales were extirpated by whaling on the European coast before A.D. 500 and on the American coast around the late 17th to early 18th centuries. The Western Pacific stock of gray whales was believed to be extinct until 1925 when a few gray whales were seen off the coast of Siberia. There are still very few sightings of these whales.

Interesting Facts: In 2011, four Pacific gray whales from Sakhalin Island, Russia, were photo-identified in Baja lagoons with the eastern Pacific population.

Two gray whale calves were captured and housed in California's Sea World in San Diego. The first (Gigi) was there from 1972-1973, and the second (J-J) from 1997-1998. Scientists gathered a great deal of information from these whales because they are the only baleen whales that have been held in captivity. The whales were released after they grew too big for their tanks.

Gray whales are the first whales in the world to be watched commercially starting in 1955 in San Diego, California for $1.00 per person.

In May 2010, a gray whale was observed in the Mediterranean Sea off Israel, and the same individual was sighted again a month later off Barcelona, Spain. It is impossible to know if this record of a single individual is indicative of a mounting reoccupation of the historic range (especially in light of receding sea ice in the Northwest and Northeast Passage) or simply represents an extraordinary event.

Gray whales were once known as "devilfish" because they fiercely defended themselves and their calves against whalers. Now in the same lagoons where they were hunted almost to extinction, gray whale mothers actually push their calves over near boats to be petted.

People commercially hunted gray whales for their oil and meat from the 17th to early 20th centuries. Today, indigenous hunters in Russia practice subsistence whaling of gray whales on a small scale.

The gray whale barnacle *Cryptolepas rhachianecti* grows only on the skin of the gray whale. The filter feeding barnacle does not feed on the whale. Rather, it sticks its feathery legs out of its shells and collects microscopic plankton from the water. These whale barnacles don't have to expend as much energy kicking their legs in and out  gathering food as a normal barnacle attached to a rock because the whale moves around, which brings plankton to them. Gray whales pick up these barnacles in the lagoons when the barnacle is in its cyprid planktonic larval stage. They grow to be about 1.5 inches.

Information sources: Primary source: NOAA. Additional sources: NMFS, Genny Anderson-SBCC, *Encyclopedia of Marine Mammals* by William F. Perrin, Bernd Würsig, J. G. M. Thewissen, Wikipedia, *Eye of the Whale* by Dick Russell, *Gray Whales: Wandering Giants* by Robert Busch, The American Cetacean Society, learner.org, sanctuarysimon.org, NIV Bible Zondervan, Mike Bursk-Ocean Institute, Robert Pittman, Edward Lyman.

Photo Information

All whale disentanglements in book were done under NOAA permits.

Cover   Brandon Cole.com/killer whale, *Orcinus orca*, attacking gray whale, *Eschrichtius robustus*/Monterey, CA

Endpapers   Composite satellite photo from space/NASA

1   Michael S. Nolan/SeaPics.com/San Ignacio Lagoon, Baja California

3   Passenger/Dolphinsafari.com/Dana Point, CA

4   David Anderson/Dana Point, CA

5   Gisele Anderson/Dana Point, CA

6-7   Mark Carwardine/Getty Images/San Ignacio Lagoon Baja California

8   David Anderson/Dana Point, CA

9-10   Andrea Swayne/*Dana Point Times*/Dana Point, CA

11-13   David Anderson/Dana Point, CA/bottlenose dolphin, *Tursiops truncatus*

14-15   Phillip Colla/SeaPics.com/Monterey, California

16U   Jeff Pantukhoff/SaveTheWhalesAgain.com/San Ignacio Lagoon, Baja California

16L   Michael S. Nolan/SeaPics.com/Magdalena Bay, Baja California

17   Mark Carwardine/Minden Pictures/Baja California

18   Marilyn & Maris Kazmers/SeaPics.com/Baja California

19   Michael S. Nolan/Getty Images/San Ignacio Lagoon, Baja California

20U   Satellite photo map/NASA

20L   David Anderson/San Ignacio Lagoon, Baja California

21   Steven Swartz/NOAA/NMFS/OPR/Baja California

22   Michael S. Nolan/SeaPics.com/San Ignacio Lagoon, Baja California

23   Brandon Cole.com/San Ignacio Lagoon, Baja California

24   Michael S. Nolan/SeaPics.com/San Ignacio Lagoon, Baja California

25   Flip Nicklin/Minden Pictures/Vancouver Island, BC, Canada

26-27   Christopher Swann/SeaPics.com/Gulf of California, Mexico

28   Kevin Schafer/Minden Pictures/San Ignacio Lagoon, Baja California

29   David Anderson/Dana Point, CA

29   Joseph Schulz/passenger on *Manute'a*/Laguna Beach, CA/Dana Point, CA

30U   NOAA/Chris Doley/Unknown

30L   David Anderson/Dana Point, CA

31   Artwork by Brien Roth/brienroth@yahoo.com 562-519-0872

32   Brandon Cole.com/San Ignacio Lagoon, Baja California

33Lft   Edward Lyman humpback whale *Megaptera novaeangliae* fluke with gillnet/Pt. Baker, AK. Mother and calf were initially entangled, but they freed themselves—NOAA Fisheries AK-PRD (MMHSRP permit #932-1905)

33Rt   Diagram-NOAA

34-35   Flip Nicklin/Minden Pictures/Vancouver Island, BC, Canada

36   Greg Hoeresty/Dana Point, CA

37U   David Anderson/Dana Point, CA

37L   Marilyn & Maris Kazmers/SeaPics.com/Magdalena Bay, Mexico

38-39L   David Anderson/Dana Point, CA

39R   Michelle Newell/Dana Point, CA

40   Brandon Cole.com/San Ignacio Lagoon, Baja California

41   David Anderson/Dana Point, CA/California sea lion, *Zalophus californianus*

42, 43, 45   David Anderson/42, 43 Dana Point, CA

44   Steve Plantz/crew/photographer *Manute'a*/Dana Point, CA

46-47   Bob Cranston/SeaPics.com/CA

48UL   David Anderson/Laguna Beach, CA/Dana Point, CA

49   Brandon Cole.com/transient killer whale/California

50-51   David Anderson

50L   Steve Plantz/crew/photographer *Manute'a*/Dana Point, CA

52   Marilyn & Maris Kazmers/SeaPics.com/Magdalena Bay, Mexico

53U   Steve Plantz/crew/photographer *Manute'a*/Dana Point, CA

53L   Alisa Schulman-Janiger/Palos Verdes, CA

54-55   Peggy Stap/SeaPics.com/Monterey, CA

56-59   Brandon Cole.com/Monterey, CA

60   Sue Flood/Minden Pictures/Monterey, CA

61   Brandon Cole.com/Monterey, CA

62   John Durban/North Gulf Oceanic Society/False Pass, AK

63   David Ellifrit/NOAA/AFSC/False Pass, AK

64-65   Flip Nicklin/Minden Pictures/Vancouver Island, BC, Canada

66   David Anderson/Dana Point, CA

67   Flip Nicklin/Minden Pictures/surfacing off of Vancouver Island, BC, Canada, with research vessel.

68-70   David Anderson/68 Juneau, AK/69L Kruzof Island, AK /70 Sitka, AK

69U   Steven Swartz/NOAA/Baja California

71   Todd Pusser/SeaPics.com/Monterey Bay, CA

72-73   David Anderson/72U St. Lazaria Island, AK/72L Kruzof Island, AK/73 Geographic Harbor, Katmai NP, AK/ brown bear, *Ursus arctos*

74-75L   David Anderson/74 Kruzof Island, AK/75L Dana Point, CA

75U   jmatzick/Shutterstock/Aleutian Islands, AK

76-77   Flip Nicklin/Minden Pictures/humpback whale with sooty shearwaters/Aleutian Islands, AK

78U   NOAA/near Unimak Island, AK

78L   Michael S. Nolan/SeaPics.com/Steller sea lion, *Eumetopias jubatus*, a threatened species/Inian Pass, Cross Sound, AK

79   Lance Barrett-Lennard/NOAA/Oksenof Pt./, Unimak Island, AK

80U   David Anderson/Pacific white-sided dolphin, *Lagenorhynchus obliquidens*/Dana Point, CA

80L   Holly Fernbach/NOAA/Aleutian Islands, AK

81   John Durban/False Pass, AK

82   Steve Plantz crew/photographer *Manute'a*/Dana Point, CA/gray whales and bottlenose dolphins interact

83   Carl Johnson/AlaskaStock.com/gillnet boat, Ugashik Bay/Bristol Bay Region, southwest AK

84   David Anderson/St. Lazaria Island, AK

85L   Aleria Jensen/NOAA Fisheries AK-PRD (MMHSRP permit #932-1489)/Ed Lyman with a gillnet-entangled humpback at the bottom of Chatham Strait, AK

85R   Howard Hall/SeaPics.com/Anacapa Island, CA

86   Flip Nicklin/Minden Pictures/Vancouver Island, BC, Canada?

87U   Satellite photo map/NASA

87L   NOAA

88-90   Staffan Widstrand/Chukchi whale hunters hunting gray whale/Chukotka, Siberia, Russia

91   David Anderson/Dana Point, CA

92-93   Staffan Widstrand/Russia Arctic/Chukotka, Siberia, Russia

94-95   Roland Seitre/SeaPics.com/Russia Arctic

96U   Michio Hoshino/Minden Pictures/near Barrow, AK

96L   NOAA/near Barrow, AK

97   Steven Kazlowski/SeaPics.com/beluga whale, *Delphinapterus leucas*/adult swims through an open lead in the pack ice during spring migration/Chukchi Sea, offshore from Barrow, AK

98U   NOAA/University of Washington/narwhal, *Monodon monoceros*/Baffin Bay, Canada

98L   Staffan Widstrand/Russia Arctic/walrus, *Odobenus rosmarus divergens*.

99   Stan Watson/Gambell, St. Lawrence Island, AK

100U   David Anderson/Dana Point, CA

100L   Michael S. Nolan/SeaPics.com/wound—note whale lice (including *Cyamus scammonii*)/San Ignacio Lagoon, Baja California

101   David Anderson/Dana Point, CA

102-103   Steven J. Kazlowski/Lefteyepro.com/near Point Barrow Chukchi Sea, AK

104   Kathy Crane/NOAA/AK Arctic

105   Steven J. Kazlowski/SeaPics.com/polar bears, *Ursus maritimus*, feeding on carcass of bowhead whale, *Balaena mysticetus*/1002 Arctic Coastal Plain of the Arctic National Wildlife Refuge, AK

106   Steven Kazlowski/Alaskastock.com/Beaufort Sea, off shore from the 1002 area of the Arctic National Wildlife Refuge, AK

107UL   David Anderson/Dana Point, CA

108-109   Flip Nicklin/Minden Pictures/Vancouver Island, BC, Canada

110   Don Paulson Photography/cruiseship/Johnstone Strait, BC, Canada

111   Steve Plantz crew/photographer *Manute'a*/Dana Point, CA

112-113U   David Anderson/112 Kruzof Island, AK/113 Sitka, AK

113L   Mark J. Rauzon/SeaPics.com/Alaskan sea otter, *Enhydra lutris kenyoni*, tangled in gillnet/Prince William Sound, AK

114   Arielle Anderson/Juneau, AK

115   Splashdown Direct/Getty Images/Orca, 'Luna' (L98): 5-year old male surfing in wake of fisheries boat/ Nootka Sound, West Vancouver Island, BC, Canada

116-117   David Anderson/Laguna Beach, CA/Dana Point, CA

118   Brian Hooker/intern on *Manute'a*, or David Anderson, not sure/Dana Point, CA

119   Dr. Harvey Barnett/Getty Images/Baja California

120-121U   David Anderson/Dana Point, CA

121U   Andrea Swayne/*Dana Point Times*/Dana Point, CA

122-123   Brandon Cole.com/San Ignacio Lagoon, Baja California

124-127   David Anderson/Dana Point, CA

128   Mark Boster/©2010 *Los Angeles Times*, reprinted with permission/Dana Point, CA

129   David Anderson/Dana Point, CA

130   Mark Tyson/Dana Point, CA

131-132   Michael Goulding/*The Orange County Register*/ Dana Point, CA

133U   KABC-TV 7/Dana Point, CA

133L-134U   David Anderson/Dana Point, CA

134L   KABC-TV 7/Dana Point, CA

135-137L   Michael Goulding/*The Orange County Register*/Dana Point, CA

137U   Barry Curtis/Dana Point, CA

138   David Anderson/Dana Point, CA

139-140U, 142   Michael Goulding/*The Orange County Register*/ Dana Point, CA

140L   David Anderson/Dana Point, CA

143   Mark Boster/© 2010 *Los Angeles Times*, reprinted with permission/Dana Point, CA

144-145   Michael S. Nolan/SeaPics.com/San Ignacio Lagoon, Baja California

146-149   David Anderson/Dana Point, CA/taken from underwater viewing pod on *Manute'a* and surface.

150   Doug Perrine/SeaPics.com/long-beaked common dolphins, *Delphinus capensis*, prey on a bait ball of sardines, *Sardinops sagax*, South Africa, during sardine run. This feeding also occurs in California and can be seen in the film *Wild Dolphins and Whales of Southern California*.

151-152U   David Anderson/Dana Point, CA/common dolphins plow through sardines/underwater viewing pod on *Manute'a*, Dana Point, CA

152L   Richard Herrmann/SeaPics.com/blue shark, *Prionace glauca*, feeding on bait ball of northern anchovies, *Engraulis mordax*/California

153   Doug Perrine/SeaPics.com/South Africa (see notes for page 150)

154   Andy Murch/SeaPics.com/shortfin mako shark, *Isurus oxyrinchus*/San Diego, CA

155   Doug Perrine/SeaPics.com/South Africa (see notes for page 150)

156   Steve Plantz/crew/photographer *Manute'a*/Dana Point, CA

157-158   David Anderson/Dana Point, CA/blue whale, *Balaenoptera musculus*

159   Barry Curtis/Laguna Beach, CA

160   Marc Carpenter/passenger on *Manute'a*/Dana Point, CA

161   David Anderson/Dana Point, CA

162U   Leslie Jeanne Morava/passenger on *Manute'a*, taken from underwater viewing pod/Dana Point, CA

162L-163   David Anderson/Dana Point, CA

164U-165   Andrea Swayne/*Dana Point Times*/Dana Point, CA

164L   David Anderson/Dana Point, CA

166-167   David Anderson/Dana Point, CA 166 taken from underwater viewing pod.

168   Steve Plantz/crew/photographer *Manute'a*/Dana Point, CA

169   David Anderson/Dana Point, CA

170L   Clarke/Faial Island, Azores Islands 1955/from coolantarctica.com

170R   Michael Goulding/*The Orange County Register*/Dana Point, CA

171   David Anderson/Dana Point, CA

172-177   David Anderson/Dana Point, CA

178   Michael S. Nolan/SeaPics.com/San Ignacio Lagoon, Baja California

179U   Steve Plantz/crew/photographer *Manute'a*/Dana Point, CA

179 L   David Anderson/Dana Point, CA

180   Jon Cornforth/SeaPics.com/San Ignacio Lagoon, Baja California

181U   David Anderson/Dana Point, CA

181L   Art Wiechmann/Laguna Beach, CA

182-185   David Anderson/Dana Point, CA

182U   Mark Tyson/Dana Point, CA

186   Michael Goulding/*The Orange County Register*/Dana Point, CA

186-187   Newspaper article by John Driscoll/ *The Times-Standard* ©2010

188   Artwork by Wyland

189   Map/from NOAA information

190   Todd Pusser/SeaPics.com/Sea World/San Diego, CA

190   Barnacled whale photo/NOAA

192   Artwork by Brien Roth/brienroth@yahoo.com 562-519-0872

Backcover U   Phillip Colla/SeaPics.com/Monterey CA

Backcover M   KABCTV-7/Dana Point CA

Backcover L   Jerry Lawlis/passenger on *Manute'a*/Dana Point, CA

Manute'a

The most unique whale watching vessel in the world

① **X-Pod©—Experimental Interspecies Communication and Underwater Viewing**

② **Micro Museum with Artifacts, Scale Models and Relics**
Whale baleen, sperm whale tooth, historic harpoons & plenty more.

③ **High Speed Engines**
Low emissions, eco-friendly with speeds up to 22 knots

④ **Underwater Research Hydrophone**
Towed hydrophone array so you can hear the dolphin's and whale's underwater sounds

⑤ **Cameras Broadcasting Live**
Every trip is broadcast LIVE on the web, conditions permitting.

⑥ **Eye-Spy Dolphin Nets**
You'll be suspended just inches over the dolphins.

⑦ **Eye-POD—Underwater Viewing Pod©**
You'll be one of the pod in this underwater area.

To learn more about
Capt. Dave's Dolphin and Whale Safari in Dana Point, CA, U.S.A.
you can go to
www. DolphinSafari.com
or call 949-488-2828

192